Intersections and ambiguity

Urban infrastructural figures of the
European Metropolis

AF086363

Fabrizia Berlingieri

Index

Perimeters 6

Infrastructure and urban form: a disciplinary framework

Position and limits

Transitions 24

State transitions: Infrastructure and urban form in XXth century
Overturns;
Duplications and Disappearences;
Substitutions

Manifesti 40

Three Paradigmatic positions of the short century
The rules of the game; Two models for a unique manifesto;
The collision between geometry and geography;
The project for the Università delle Calabrie;
Architectural singularity and infrastructural iperurbanity;
Euralille a dislocated city

Contemporary morphotypes 70

A conflicting relation. Infrastructural morphotypes & the contemporary urban scene of the European Metropolis
The Divided Ground; The Basement; The Platform

A space for design: intersections and ambiguity

Architectural perspectives on Infrastructures and City; three accounts 98

Roberto Cavallo

acknowledgments

This book constitutes a reviewed and expanded collection of essays written during the Post Doc research on *Emerging urban forms in European geography. Potential and project for urban complex systems involved in the infrastructural reorganization of the European Space*. The research was developed between 2011 and 2013 at the Università Mediterranea di Reggio Calabria and at the TU Delft, Faculty of Architecture and the Built Environment. I sincerely thank the supervisors and professors Laura Thermes, Tom Avermaete and Roberto Cavallo for their constant and precise attention. Further thanks to Serafina Amoroso and Manuela Triggianese with whom I shared and developed many arguments of the research.

In fact, it is undoubtedly difficult to define with an acceptable approximation what are infrastructures.
The name identifies them as interstitial and pervasive realities, technical entities that in any case place a presence in space that exceeds their role. They are, at the same time, works of engineering and architecture, but also take part of the landscape dimension, establishing themselves as elements of an artificial geography, often quite substantial.

Franco Purini,
Questioni di Infrastrutture, 2005

Perimeters

Infrastructure and urban form: a disciplinary framework

The interdependence between urban settlement and infrastructural presence within the dynamics of landscape transformations distinguishes an important and plural area of contemporary debate in Architecture. It moves from the observation of a constant acceleration of territorial mutations in recent decades, setting their backbone on infrastructural systems, physical and unphysical, and coagulating around them new forms of dwelling whose thrust takes consistency from a specific *condition of reciprocity*. The plurality of these positions bases its common ground on an *infrastructure's conceptual instability*[1]. Infrastructure, indeed, cannot be understood as a mere technical matter only related to the needs and rules of Transport Engineering, but on the contrary as a causal element of deep settlement modifications, far from its original image of a *connecting line*[2] between two entities.
The cross-over of meanings that this uncertain statute has reached in last decades can be resumed in a general framework composed by three specific approaches, in which contemporary research and design experiences can be addressed.

The first one places itself around the recent sociological reflections on the economic and political changes occurred at the new millennium's beginning[3]. The alarming implementation of a macroeconomic scale able to rewrite the nation-states' role and their geographies on a global scale has generated a new interpretative model, the *network system*, which takes shape in an emerging process of territorial hierarchic organization. Places acquire importance and centrality due to a heavy infrastructural presence and to the consequent ability to be connected with the whole, gaining a privileged position with the status of *edge cities*[4]. As result of a continuous trading between scales and multiple actors, the contemporary urban horizon is outlined as *blurred figure*, composed by masses of critical density held together by an infrastructural network of communication:

«real networked territories, where each pole is defined as a point of intersection and switching of multiple nets, as a dense node in a giant web of flows which is the only reality.[5]»

As unstable thickenings, they seem to fit into *another* space, overwritten to the physical palimpsest of reality, spreading transnational connections[6]. The transposition of these reflections, within the architectural discipline, takes place in a renewed focus on the geographical dimension, pushing research speculations on *connections' representability*. The main objective consists of visualizing ties, tracks and relations generated by infrastructures able to describe, through the tool of diagrammatic *mapping*, the characters of a territorial system as mirror of the political and economic one: changing, fluid, unstable[7]. In such visions infrastructure assumes the meaning of connection devoid of physicality, a virtual element generating cartographic oxymorons that are based on a *relational thickness*. Beyond the assignment of an *abstract value* of infrastructures, other studies investigate how this trans-local condition affect social practices in metropolitan contexts, where this process *makes space within infrastructures*[8]. However, very often, the diagrammatic character of these transcriptions in the architectural discipline reveals a double risk: on the one hand, showing a sort of critical resignation about the conditions imposed by the "global model" and, on the other, lessening the impact that these junctions produce in physical urban dimension. Arises, indeed, a problem of *materialization of new settlement morphologies*, linked to the flow dynamics, which frequently overlap themselves on the stratified frame of territories, generating ambiguous complicities, if not outright conflicts.

«Rather these new forms and those inherited from history seem to be able to live within new frameworks of meaning that hide, under the blanket of an apparent familiarity of the daily scene settlement, the multiple and disjoint memberships to the space of flows and the new scales of interdependence with territories at a distance. Thus new settlement morphologies accompany the profound changes that have affected the places of living, producing, consuming and their specific relationships.[9]»

The second approach revolves around the American researches developed in the sixties and seventies[10], on new ways of urban readings, formal and iconographic, based on the observation and the description of the open space *through* infrastructures as main tools of landscape perception. The design methodology is explicated through the concept of *scenic sequences*, based on an *interior view* where the infrastructure becomes a narrative voice, a conveyor belt of the aesthetic experience through the city[11]. According to this direction, contemporary infrastructural landscape design, that focuses on the construction of routes scenarios, as well as on punctual interventions belonging to the scenic construction of an artificial landscape.

«An experiment, (...), which consists of localized attention, episodic, linked to problems very well circumscribed, in which infrastructure is treated to individual fragments where unfolds the narrative dimension of architecture, most often through a series of operations of detail, adaptations to the context, landscape insertions.[12]»

The remodeling of a visual and perceptive experience "of the exterior, from the road"[13] becomes a dominant logic through which the design of infrastructural systems is now rethought in terms of collective identity[14]. In this second area of study, the materiality of the infrastructure and its physical concreteness, in relation to the changes that inevitably generates, seem to have a secondary role. Indeed design strategies are intended as tools for the deployment of territorial aesthetic values, in which the role of the architectural project is confined to reinvent borders, horizons and perspectives in a space substantially unurbanized or, on the contrary, taking back the same values in the urbanized ones, directing the infrastructural project to a totalizing landscape dimension. This approach has been reinforced by the issue of environmental sustainability, in which the search for a new balance between nature and infrastructure often undergoes artificial mystifications[15].

The third approach, that the research tracks within the complexity of the disciplinary framework, recognizes a typo- morphological discourse that considers infrastructure as a physical element weaving precise material relationships with the context. It is characterized by a disciplinary cross-border that refers to radical positions, to in the experiences of the sixties and seventies in England, France and Italy, grouped in the concepts of *Megastructural poetic* or *Territorial Architecture*, although with meaningful differences[16]. The *fil rouge* of these experiences, geographically spread-out and sometimes even conflicting in results, can be traced in an implicit continuity of the role of infrastructure between the morphological dimension of architecture and the distributive one of planning, framing the design tools within an action area conceptually applicable, in a progressive enlargement of scale, to the whole environment[17]. The infrastructure, in this sense, takes the form of a territorial architecture, according to which the infrastructural project draws its strength in recognizing the open scene by providing with its presence the narrative dimension that was before prerogative of urban forms. In this line are recognizable two research and design branches, which do not shy away from some contemporary overlaps. The first, on urban planning, considers infrastructure as the ordering principle of space and the cornerstone of anthropological changes[18], while the second considers, with a more proper architectural reading, infrastructure as an *artifact* that involves the sphere of design through a spatial approach.

«There are clearly two different aspects which are connecting infrastructure, territory and architecture, two aspects closely linked, but somehow also separable. The first considers infrastructure as trace, visible or invisible, in which the consequences on territories' geographies are key elements of the mutations involved by their paths as well as for settlement aspects, contrasts, incentives or demolitions. The second aspect concerns the design of the manufact, its ability to dialogue with the surrounding, its conjugation between structural invention, architectural form and context, its crossings between the natural and the artificial, or the ability to measure its own scale with the surrounding urban environment.[19]»

The key given by this research lies at the intersection of these values, assuming the semantic duplicity of infrastructure as formal *archetype* and spatial principle.

Position and limits

«During the twentieth century urbanization has replaced the millenary process of construction of the city. The classical concept of the urban nucleus as a formal structure is out of date. (...). There have been significant changes in both form and character of urbanization due to the large infrastructure projects related to transports.[20]»

The "making space" of infrastructural systems into consolidated urban structures or in territories largely urbanized requires an urgent and critical reflection within the disciplinary area, about how these "junctions" occur, as well as how to redraw their precise configurations in the crowded contemporary scene. The attempt offered by a morphological approach[21], even if it comes in a time of deep rethinking on the possibilities of analyzing urban phenomena, recognizes a continuous dynamic of balance between permanence and evolution in the shared construction of the city[22].

«Urban design means that the architecture starts out from data to be found in the city -remains, memories, fragments, guidelines- choosing them in a selective manner as constraints in its own design, the moment that this is proposed as a response and solution to a state of things that had already been perceived as incomplete, disjointed, unresolved. The reliance on this mode of operating in relation to what exists, to history, to the city already built, is considered important and often has repercussions on the innovative character of such architecture. With a fair degree of sophistication, and with a certain disciplinary indulgence, the city is interpreted as topography and concrete location, as existing reference, as tradition and continuity.[23]»

Rather than defending an interdisciplinary approach, the research opposes an attempt to reconstruct the current debate on infrastructure from an architectural point of view, aiming to understand its semantic relations, its figurative possibilities, its translations onto forms. The narration starts from a critical review of the settlement *models* with which urban design has been in comparison dialogically until a few decades ago, while the body of this research is divided into two main chapters. The first, *Manifesti*, analyzes the theoretical panorama between First and Second Modernism, through the critical reading of three models considered "prophesies" of the changes in urban and territorial transformations of the last century, and their considerable influence on contemporary design. The three models have been investigated considering both the theoretical and the design apporaches.

The second part of the study on contemporary morphotypes focuses, through a "cross section" of projects, on the critical analysis of infrastructural projects related to the process of spatial reorganization of the European metropolis. Contemporary large scale interventions, leading ongoing transformation processes of main world cities, are often related to mobility systems. Developed around the reconversion or the implementation of infrastructural nodes, they deeply impact surrounding areas within a more general rethinking of urban conditions. However, the relation between urbanity and infrastructure appears at least ambiguous. On the one hand mobility flows represent key components and engines for transformations, on the other their physical presence progressively disappears from the urban scene itself. Starting from this observation the chapter proposes a reflection on the status of a *conflicting relation*, recognizing in which ways these hidden infrastructures are actually reshaping the contemporary city scape.

The geographical scale of analysis and critical reading, both for settlement models and for contemporary scenarios, are related to the European context. This perimeter stands as a first limit, which is at the same time spatial and cultural. The belief, indeed, is that this choice is coherent in referring to a centuries-old tradition of urban construction, made not by the set up of individuals iconic elements, but through that of the urban scene, in the coexistence of tissues and monuments, such as in the modeling of an urban form through the definition of the collective void.

«European cities have deep historical roots to the point that they cannot allow to be cut by an uncontrolled modernization, entrusted to mere financial dynamics of the building cycle. (...). The Forma Urbis of historic cities has settled not only a physical structure of social space, but also a constellation of intangible cultural values and collective symbols that guides civil society.[24]»

The research does not circumscribe on a single mode of transport - rail, highway, air or sea - just because often the strategies of engagement between infrastructure and urban body are not really exclusively attributable to the transport typology. Although certainly influencing, they seem to depend more on a *figurative irreconcilability*, increasingly more and more evident in the last decades. Another limit of the research, somehow mentioned above, is regarding Modernism as a temporal reference, articulating the critical inquiry only on the last two centuries. The thesis argues that the relationship between infrastructure and urban form, described in the contemporary scene as "dusty system", is actually the ultimate consequence of a deep split of urban scene's unity right occurred in Modernism. The advent of infrastructure as a new and independent figure, competitor and antagonist in composing the whole of the urban reality, has contributed decisively to the future development of European territories. And perhaps from this figure is necessary to re-start for finding design tools and strategies with which to compare consciously the current urgencies of speculative urbanizations, in the attempt of repositioning the role of architecture as the main agent of stress for future.

1. "The term *Infrastructure* comes from the latin compound *infra* and *structure*: the prefix *infra*, "which is under", was semantically confused in late period with *intra*, "inside". Infra is first element of modern formed compounds, meaning "lower, below, inner." Infrastructure, therefore, as hierarchical below structure, subject to other arrangement, secondary." Devoto, G.; Oli, G.C .(1971). *Dizionario della Lingua Italiana*. Firenze: Le Monnier.

2. Important positions, related to infrastructure as connecting line, were present at the beginning of the twentieth century, emphasizing its distributive and formal values:

"Unlike architectural works in strict sense, bridges don't shape space, but cross it, they don't serve to delimit, but to connect. Their function is to cover a hollow, connecting two points through a linear system." In Hilberseimer, L. (1927). *Großstadt Architektur*. Stuttgart: Julius Hoffmann Verlag; ed. it. (1988). *L'architettura della grande città*. Milano: Clean.

"The men who first drew a road between two places carried out one of the most important achievements. They could have come and gone between the two, so to make them unified, but only when they imprinted on the surface of the earth the road, those places were united objectively, the will had become Form of things, form that was offered to the will for each repetition without depending on its frequency or scarcity." In Simmel, G. (1903). *Ponte e Porta*. In: Cacciari, M.; Perucchi, L. (edited by), (1970). *Saggi di Estetica*. Padova: Cedam.

3. Castells, M. (1989). *The Informational City*. Oxford; Blackwell, Sassen, S. (1994). *Cities in a World Economy*. New York: Pine Forge Press.

4. Garreau, J. (1991). *Edge cities. Life on the new frontier*. New York: Anchor Books.

5. Veltz, P. (1996). *Les lieux et les liens. Politique du territoire à l'heure de la modialisation*. Paris: Presses Universitaires de France.

6. Graham, S.; Marvin, S. (2001). *Splintering Urbanism. Networked infrastructures, technological mobilities and the urban condition*. London: Routledge.

7. Bauman, Z. (2000). *Liquid Modernity*. Cambridge: MIT Press.

8. Desideri, P.; Ilardi, M., edited by (1997). *Attraversamenti. I nuovi territori dello spazio pubblico*. Milano. Costa & Nolan.

9. Clementi, A. (2010). Territorio: una risorsa per lo sviluppo. *XXI Secolo*, Treccani on line. www.treccani.it.

10. Appleyard, D.; Lynch, K.; Myer, J. (1964). *The view from the Road*. Cambridge: MIT Press, e Venturi, R.; Scott Brown, D.; Izenour, S. (1972). *Learning from Las Vegas*. Cambridge: MIT Press.

11. "This is established from the point of view of the real user, sociologically defined, without envisaging the problem of the historicity of this perception, or with regard to its change over the time, either regarding its positional relationship in the cultural model." Gregotti, V. (1966). *Il territorio dell'architettura*. Milano. Feltrinelli.

12. Privileggio, N. (2006). Infrastruttura, architettura: Alcune precisazioni. *Files*, arch'it. www.archit.it.

13. Calabrese, L.M.; Houben, F.; edited by (2003). *Mobility: a room with a view*. Rotterdam: Nai Publishers.

14. Lassus, B. (1998), *The Landscape Approach*. Philadelphia: University of Pennsylvania Press.

15. Shannon, K.; Smets, M.; edited by (2010). *The Landscape of Contemporary Infrastructure*. Rotterdam: Nai Publishers.

16. "Since the sixties, the term *megastructure* indicates complexes not necessarily as extensive as extensible, usually set to a fixed structure and smaller units removable. Features are the multi-function (fusion of accommodation units, jobs, services, leisure) and of course a high technology (...)." Pevsner, N. (1981). *Dizionario di architettura*. Torino: Einaudi. Early studies of this poetic were developed in 1964 by Fumijiko Maki, that formulated a first definition, and later systematized in the volume of Reyner, B. (1976). *Megastructure: Urban Futures of Recent Past*. London: Thames and Hudson. In this text the author attempts to codify, or rather to organize, the different positions of this trend, depending on the geographical origin and the cultural assumptions, that were interested in the new issue of a territorial dimension.

17. "This is an exploration together on the consistency and on the extension of our disciplinary borders, but also is about the possible contribution to its further development, which may result from focusing on the issue of an architectural solution of those problems; it is about offering the specificity of our disciplinary tradition to their quality organization and, at the same time, to acquire methods and points of view to the architectural design that can capture new aspects; finally it is about emphasizing not only the responsibility but the structural nature of architecture as a physical modification and sense of the relations, not only regarding their changes with the environment, but as the

product itself of an intentioned relational thinking." Gregotti, V. (1989). La strada: tracciato e manufatto. *Casabella*, 553-554. Milano: Casabella Edizioni.

18. Secchi, B. (2005). Figure della mobilità. *Casabella*, 739-740. Milano: Electa.

19. Gregotti, V. (2012). Il territorio delle infrastrutture. In Ferlenga, A.; Albrecht, B.; Biraghi, M.; edited by (2012). *L'Architettura del Mondo. Infrastrutture, mobilità, nuovi paesaggi*. Catalogue of the Milano Triennale Exhibition. Firenze: Editrice Compositori.

20. Ingersoll, R. (2010). La proliferazione della città. *XXI Secolo*, Treccani on line. www.treccani.it. On the polisemic condition of the meaning of urban structure see also Ingersoll, R. (2004). *Sprawltown, cercando la città in periferia*. Roma: Meltemi Editore.

21. In particular, the research reference address the Italian theoretical panorama of Second Modernism. For more precise reconstructions of the debate and its protagonists see the essay "The language and the notion of scale in the modernist urban project" in Thermes, L. (2000). *Tempi e Spazi, scritti teorici. La città e il suo progetto nella età posturbana*. Roma: Diagonale Editore; either the text of Marzot, N. (2002). The study of urban form in Italy. *Urban Morphology*, 6 (2).

22. Purini, F. (1976). *Luogo e Progetto*. Roma: Magma Editrice.

23. De Solà Morales, I. (2001). Territori. *Lotus*, 110. Milano: Industrie Grafiche Editoriali.

24. Gravagnuolo, B. (2010). La modificazione della città europea. *XXI Secolo*, Treccani on line. www.treccani.it.

0.1

0.2

0.3

0.6

0. Università della Calabria.
Arcavacata - Rende (1974/1994)

Masterplan design: Gregotti Associati.
Competition team (1974): Vittorio Gregotti, Emilio Battisti, Hiromichi Matsui, Pierluigi Nicolin, Franco Purini, Carlo Rusconi Clerici e Bruno Viganò.

Images credits

0.1-0.2 Under the bridge

0.3 Departments and the interior space of the bridge

0.4 Università della Calabria, the second level (pedestrian) of the bridge

0.5 Università della Calabria, the first level of the bridge

0.6 Università della Calabria, top view

source: Fabrizia Berlingieri

Transitions

State transitions: Infrastructure and urban form in XXth century

Overturns
At the turn of the nineteenth century the last consequences of the Industrial Revolution subvert the city in the final dismantling of its ancient boundaries, dissolving it into the open by means of a new system of communication. This deep physical change is followed by a constant research of a proper and original iconography, able to represent aims and desire of the growing industrial society, assuming progress as a leitmotif of a new metropolitan vision. It's a hundred thousand inhabitants city (1801. *Plan d'une ville pour cent mille ames*. Jean Jacque Moll); a linear city as infinite locomotive that runs in the bucolic countryside (1862. *Ciudad Lineal*. Sorya y Mata); a limitless metropolis that concentrically subjugates an abstract geographic space, finally conquered by the immeasurable extension of roads network (1904. *The Limitless Metropolis*, O. Wagner); a cluster of mechanical gears (1914. *Città Nuova*. Antonio Sant'Elia). This new image does not recognize cultural differences or historical roots. It's a unique voice that requires to its authors the concretion of a pre-global time original vision, characterized by the presence of a new *figure*, the infrastructure, which exceeds definitely the image of the *street*[1]. Following the diverse proposals that succeed feverishly in those years, the infrastructural figure takes different meanings: it is a stable structure, a backbone (1910. *Roadtown*. Edward Chambless), a main vocation (1924. *Citè de Circulation*. Theo Van Doesburg), a physical measure's unity (1924. *Die Grosstadt*. Ludwig Hilberseimer).
The deep change at the beginnings of XXth century, that will be stigmatized along Modernism, comes clear: the city of the XXth century *is* the city of infrastructures, of communication networks that will replace the human scale in favor of the mechanized one, establishing a first *state transition*. The unity of the urban scene, built on the interdepence between void and

mass, between the street and the building, is substituted by the figurative autonomy of singular elements[2]. The spatial urban scene defined by continuous built curtains[3] is overpassed by an openness horizon, in which nature and artifice become interrelated components. Finally the transposition of the Modern Architecture's general principles of the free architectural plan is achieved at urban scale. In this semantic overturn, in the reversal of urban scene's composition, transport system becomes the main actor:

«Centralization, decentralization: this is the substantial difference between ancient and modern city, and is necessary to ask if this transformation is possible through mere demolitions, as in the Haussmann boulevards.(...). Characters of the ancient cities are beauty and tranquility; but the modern city is not more an open air museum, a sculpture and architecture exhibition. The quiet and contemplative life of the past is replaced by the speed, the noise and mechanics of advertising.[4]»

The urban development linked to industrialization and the process of formal autonomy reorganize meanings and role of infrastructure within urbanity, transforming the city, at the turn of twentieth century, in a *system of objects* floating in dialogue through distance. It's an *exploded space*[5], a city carefully dismantled and lying into the open, where each element acquires autonomy of form and becomes singular presence.
In this homogeneous space the memories of the ancient cities with the new metropolitan archetypes lie together: the tertiary towers dominate the horizon, the redents are merged with the green profile, again, the infrastructure looks as a long isolated ribbon. These characters of the modern city as resulting effect of dismantling the urban scene unity, the gigantism, the spatial

isotropy generate what Sitte defined as the *disease of modern isolation*[6].

Duplications and Disappearances
Along the Second Modernism Louis Kahn leads the research on city's invariants to extreme consequences, as it is presented in the *Philadelphia Masterplan* of 1953. The cruciform skyscrapers of LC, as punctuation of the Cartesian grid, are substituted by formal archetypes - cylinders, cones, pyramids - closely disposed. They introduce the lost of spatial isotropy tanks to the presence of a gravitational dialogue, a *spatial difference* that attempts to a possible resematicization of the road and its social role:

«The road is a room that expresses a deal. In today's cities the dead-end streets still retain the character of the room. The crossing roads, since the advent of the car, have lost at all the quality of the room. I believe that urbanism can begin by becoming aware of this loss and trying to reinstall the street, where people live, learn, buy and work, in its role of community room[7].»

The idea of *community room* is a main theme of the researches on the relationship between infrastructure and urban form carried by Robert Venturi and Kevin Lynch[8]. The perspective of human eye is substituted by the rear mirror of the automobile, in which the Las Vegas' strips, with neon signs and empty spaces of crossing, become new elements of a diffuse urbanity accessible only by car[9]. The characters of internity and dynamism definitively push the meaning of infrastructure in the post war economic boom of sixties and seventies:

«Much has been written on circulation - of its mechanical and numerical connotations - too often was considered abstractly, as an urban function between others. The circulation, however, cannot be completely understood in terms of function

(...). Transport is one particular aspect of communication, communication a particular aspect of mobility in general. Today mobility is not any aspect of life in cities, but it is made of the very essence of human relationships, while in theory the city should provide the framework for human relations in their most diverse and complex form[10].»

The reflection of Aldo Van Eyck announces a *second state transition*: the passage from the idea of *infrastructure* as constitutive element of modern urban space, equal and autonomous component, to a new concept of relational vector of a general system of mobility. It is, according to the architect, an *identifying device of a new urbanity* and more precisely of its expansion towards an *open form*. In the same direction proceeds the research of Alison and Peter Smithson that founded a specific design iconography about the infrastructure and its role in contemporary urban development, as the project for *Golden Lane Housing* in London of 1952 and *Haupstadt Berlin* of some years later demonstrate[11]. In Smithson's experimental projects the settlement design literally duplicates the infrastructural one. The city seems to be the overlapped simulation of circulation flows, becoming a sort of iconic network mold. Even in the work of the Italian group Superstudio, with an opposite result, the concept of general mobility is translated in the *disappearance* of the urban structure in favor of an homologous Cartesian plan of individual human trajectories. In an opposite image, the urban scene, *where there will be no need for streets and squares*[12], is for Superstudio the abandonment of a spatial fixity, substituted by an infinite and neutral social space. Between these two opposite visions emerges the role of infrastructure as *principle of spatial distribution*. Infrastructural networks, perhaps the only example of mega-structure actually realized, become principle of spatial normalization, as necessary support to the speculative use of the territory in a social system essentially based on communication.

Another Italian research branch, focusing on the constant acceleration of settlements development dynamics, proposes a different conceptual framework that has in the *unity between architecture and urbanism* its instrument, a disciplinary inflection point between architecture, infrastructure and territory[13]. It is an interstitial research area in which the boundaries between the dimension of urban plan and the architectural one become uncertain, up to intersect themselves in an *intermediate level*. This interrelation between form, structure and scale refers to the dimension of *territorial architecture*:

«If then one arises to a great distance, in the synthesis of the map, in an aerial vision for example, things lose recognizability, however enforcing our possibilities to understand their structure; things reduce themselves to points, to plugs; the whole of points and plugs gives the texture on the ground, modalities and directions according its institution; the margin lines of tangency, of conflict, the entire parts and the rests, the collision between geometry and geography[14].»

In this zenith eye-view the reading and the perceptibility of architectural intentions necessarily suffer a scalar expansion, dealing with geographic coordinates. The *collision between geometry and geography* represents the common issue of a methodological proceeding in balance between the repeatability of a model and the recovery of a compositive dimension formally concluded even on the larger scale. This attempt specifies a qualitative difference of the Italian research respect to other experiences outside national borders. While, indeed, the megastructural researches attempt to reveal the gears of the industrial society on a new global scale, the Italian experience tries to control the extension of these machines, measuring architectural objects in relation to the context, defining proper limits and specific identity.

Substitutions

The last decades of XXth century have been characterized by a pluri-directioned research on the relation between infrastructure and urban form. Some specific research areas can be distinguished within this plurality of voices and protagonists. Even with different outcomes, they start from the common ground of a definitive abandonment of a visionary ideality on city's future that results in discrete models, as occasions of pragmatic experimentations. Since the end of the eighties, indeed, under the premonition of the Berlin Wall fall, the lights of the European capital cities were pointed on voids left by the race to expansion, residual areas often linked to infrastructural traces. Simultaneously to the rethinking of metropolitan *cores* through acupuncture strategies, peripheries continued undisturbed their exponential growth along the same infrastructural lines. So at the turn of the new millennium, the old continent wakes up with a different face, permanently changed under the development impetus of a new polycentric model, that pushes its gravity center towards the north-european axis. Within these trajectories, some models can be underlined to describe the contemporary horizon, inextricably linked to the antagonism between settlement development and infrastructural appetite. A third *state transition*, that inscribes the evolution of infrastructural space as the *substitutive replica* of urban structure. The issue of inhabiting infrastructural space grounds on the predominant temporal model of contemporary that has in the transport network its own community room, with a consequently important evolution in typological researches. The interrelation between the space of flows and the space of dwelling gives form to a relation that has been a recently privileged field of research. But, if in Modernism, this issue was investigated by means of a radical re-foundation of settlement values and forms, nowadays its condition appears really different:

«the today's architecture of infrastructures, in opposition to Kahn's hypothesis, tends to abandon the technique of collage and also the references to the consolidated urban fabric, preferring the commistion of parts and hybrid figures, towards a synthetic form and in parallel trying to express the internal conflicts existing in each kind of space based on mass mobility[15].»

This trend leads to a phenomenon of *city's reduction to infrastructural macrospaces*, where the imagery of the city is reconstructed as a *simulacrum* within the complex, pervasive and enveloping system of transport networks. In opposition to Modernism and Megastructural poetics, today the narrative dimension is denied in favor of an immediacy that leaves no space for conflicting interpretations[16]. It's a *fragile dwelling*, made of continuous relations, constantly addressing connections between different parts, scales, uses and functions of territories. Beyond the concept of metropolis, where it is still possible to think of urban settlement as a coordinated whole of different parts, European city no longer has a center or a predefined direction. Quoting Cacciari, the contemporary EUCity shows itself as a space-time continuous structure where:

«the system of reference could be anyone; the distribution of matter changes continuously and without advices; where don't govern the Clock and the Rule; where bodies and languages deform themselves during the flox; where, consequently, movement plays an active role in defining the form of the objects, the time is not a riverbed in which things run (relations, connections, languages, forms) but it is those things[17].»

According to this vision, the city is understood as extensive system where the infrastructure represents the most emblematic dwelling dimension.

1. Sitte, C. (1945), *The Art of Building Cities:Building according to its artistic fundamentals.* Mansfield centre, CT: Martino Publ. (ed. or.1889 Vienna: Graeser).

2. In the mechanical montage takes place, in the early twentieth century, the gradual overturning of the unity of form and uniqueness of reproduction, a process common to arts and technology described by Walter Benjamin in his essay, *The Art at the age of its technical reproducibility*, 1936. The subsequent act of resemanticization of the linguistic code in architecture, led by the De Stijl movement, is detected by Bruno Zevi as invariant of modernity, in the volume *The Language of modern architecture. Guide to the anticlassical code*, 1973. However, a precedent of the unit fall already appears in the work of the architects of french revolution, as analyzed by Emil Kaufmann, in his essay *From Ledoux to Le Corbusier. Origins and development of autonomous architecture* in 1933.

3. Sebastiano Serlio, *Scena Tragica*, 1500. Scenography present in the II book of the treaty Sebastiano Serlio, *I sette Libri dell'Architettura*, 1537.

4. Theo Van Doesburg *Cité de Circulation*, 1924. In Zevi, B.(1974). *Poetica dell'architettura neoplastica.* Torino: Einaudi.

5. Choay, F. (ed.it.: 2000). *La città: utopie e realtà.* Torino: Einaudi.

6. Sitte, C. (1889). *Op.cit.*

7. Louis Kahn, *Plan for Philadelphia. Project report*, 1953. In Ghersi, F. (2008). *Scritti sulla Modernità.* Cannitello: Biblioteca del Cenide.

8. Lynch, K. (1960) *The image of the city.* Cambridge: MIT Press; Venturi, R; Scott Brown, D.; Izenour, S. (1972). *Learning from Las Vegas.* Cambridge: MIT Press.

9. Banham, R. (ed.it.: 2000). *Architettura della seconda età della Macchina.* Milano: Electa.

10. Aldo Van Eyck, *Passi verso una disciplina configurativa*, 1962. In Biraghi, M.; Damiani, G.; a cura di (2009). *Le parole dell'architettura. Un'antologia di testi teorici e critici: 1945-2000.* Torino: Einaudi, pp. 75-99.

11. Risselada, M.; van den Heuvel, D. eds (2006). *Team 10. In search of a Utopia of the present 1953-1981.* Rotterdam: NAI010 publishers.

12. Superstudio, *Un viaggio tra A e B: non ci sarà più bisogno di strade né piazze*, 1969.

13. In this direction, even with some differences, should be addressed the research and experimentations conducted by Giancar-

lo De Carlo, Ludovico Quaroni, Giuseppe Samona, that will have in the generation represented by Vittorio Gregotti and Franco Purini, among others, following outcomes. The project experiences focus on stable issues and strategies: the recovery of figurative unit against the open dimension of urban design, the architectural gigantism, the value of urban architectural design againt the one of planning.

14. Gregotti, V. (II ed.: 1975). *Il territorio dell'architettura*. Milano: Feltrinelli, p. 82.

15. Mosco, V.P. «L'architettura delle infrastrutture», in Maffioletti, S.; edited by (2005). *I Paesaggi delle infrastrutture*. Padova: Il Poligrafo, p.106.

16. «The thesis extremes on the disappearance of the importance of physical space in the city as recognizable identity, and the deployment of the immaterial space of urban living as a virtual city, an idea supported by a major study of e-topie (...). But it is clear that the city of networks is something outstanding, without limits and center, something that no longer refers to a ground, to the idea of founding, to that of site instead of its intangible relationships.» Gregotti, V. (2011). *Architettura e Postmetropoli*. Torino: Einaudi.

17. Massimo Cacciari, Metropoli della mente, 1986. In Biraghi, M.; Damiani, G. (2009). *Le parole dell'architettura. Un'antologia di testi teorici e critici: 1945-2000*. Torino: Einaudi, pp. 446-453.

1. Euralille project. Lille (1989-1994)

Masterplan design: OMA, Rem Koolhaas; Floris Alkemade; Donald van Dansik

Images credits
1.1 Euralille, Boulevard de Turin/Parvis de Rotterdam. Lille Tower (left), former Tour du Crédit-Lyonnais built above Lille-Europe railway station. Arch. Christian de Portzamparc, 1991-95.
source: Fred Romero (flickr, CC)

1.2 Gare Lille-Europe, Place François-Mitterrand, High speed trains railway station. Arch. Jean-Marie Duthilleul 1994.
source: Fred Romero (flickr, CC)

1.3 Gare Lille-Europe, métro de Lille Métropole
source: maxdufour (flickr, CC)

1.4 Lille commercial center
source: Yacine Petitprez (flickr, CC)

According to the slogan "hubs for urban life" the new plan was presented the first masterplan drawn up in 2001 by Alsop, later rejected and remodeled according to the principles of a greater feasibility by Maxwan Architects in 2004. The project is developed around the new intermodal station and, in a logic of continuity with the building densification of the area, is provided the completion of urban curtain with new high rise buildings, redefining the image of the city from the rail.

The program - partly already realized as the new station by Team CS (Benthem Crouwel, Meijer & Van Schooten and West 8), the private building mixed-use Calypso by William Alsop and the renovation of Central Post by Kees Kaan - schedules its completion in 2020 with the construction of a road tunnel for the new external plaza near several station and the surrounding buildings completing a new skyline for the city of Rotterdam.

2. Rotterdam Central District, Mixone. Rotterdam (2007/2020)

Masterplan design: Maxwan architects and Urbanists + Municipality of Rotterdam with Department of Urban Design (dS+V) and Land Development Rotterdam (OBR)

Images credits

2.1 Rotterdam central station district. The private building mixed-use Calypso by William Alsop

2.2 Rotterdam central station. Team CS (Benthem Crouwel, Meijer & Van Schooten and West 8)

2.3 Rotterdam waterfront and Erasmus Bridge

source: Fabrizia Berlingieri

2.4 The Central station, Rotterdam, The Netherlands
source: Ira Smirnova, (flickr, CC)

Manifesti

Three paradigmatic positions of the short century

The rules of the game
In 1922, commenting the *Diorama of a Contemporary City* at the Paris Salon d'Automne, Le Corbusier wrote:

«Wanting to preserve anachronistic old plans means to paralyze urban development. (...) The conservative criteria applied to large cities prevent the transport evolution, cause traffic congestion, slow down the life rhythm, are fatal to progress, to any initiative.[1]»

The main assumption, underlying the theoretical formulations of LC, moves from the observation of a necessary re-foundation of modern urbanism: the twentieth century is a time and a space based on circulation, in which the city claims for a structural resemanticization[2]. In the opening chapter of *Urbanisme* «Les chamins des anes e les chamins des hommes», LC states the end of the street in its intrinsic value of void within the built fabric. It is substituted by the concept of *tracé régulateure*, a new autonomous entity described in the final part of the same volume as fundamental component of the project for a *Contemporary City of three million inhabitants*. The observation of the needs that accompany the growing social demand of industrial society, gives way to a laboratory experiment for the development of a universal *prototype*, objective, scientific:

«Working in the manner of the laboratory expert, I avoided the specific cases, neglected all the incidental details, to give me an ideal breeding ground. The aim was not to overcome the existing, but to get to formulate the basic principles to the modern urbanism, organizing them into a theoretical building of extreme rigor. These principles, if they are not counterfeit, may constitute the backbone of the entire system of contemporary urbanism: the rule of the game.[3]»

The *rule of the game* consists of the functional reorganization of modern life translated in precise design issues: the *density* related to the recognition of different architectural types of dwelling; the *artificialization of nature* recaptured to the city as provision of leisure equipment; the circulation, finally, acquiring three- dimensionality and depth as structural framework, once freed from the physical constraint of the urban tissue.

«A sort of fabric developed in length, an aerate storehouse where are collected many complex and delicate organisms. This fabric's plan presents diverse destinations, according to the traits. Its realization is equal, in fact, to one of housing that normally flank it, of the bridges that prolong its course through the valleys or from one river side to the other. The modern street must be a creation of civil construction and no more a digger's work.[4]»

LC approaches the *circulation model* not only as trace but as artifact, investigating its formal and spatial characters in the range of architectural construction. Its type-morphological consistency is fully described in the *Athens Charter* by means of typical sections that list conditions of use, functions and vertical hierarchies in the spatial articulation of its figure[5]. In a parallel way LC implements the codification of his *urban alphabet*[6], made up of few elements. A *design's taxonomy*, in which the repetition of the singular codified pieces of the city - redents, skyscrapers, industrial pavilions, infrastructural circuits- joins the research for their possible variation in a dialogue with the landscape, disclosing the environmental specificities. The enlargement of the infrastructural role on the scale of landscape characterizes a new vision of LC about territorial systems in which infrastructure becomes a *complex framework*. In his text *Sur Les Quatre Routes*, the theoretical reflections are extended to all transport modalities - air, railway, highway and sea-, later converging in *Les Trois Etablissements Humains* and in *Manière de penser l'urbanisme*. In these last researches LC turns the attention on the relation between infrastructure and settlement systems in a more general model, prefigured as three city-types constellations, linear, agricol and radio-centric. The three-type settlement model stands out as extendible network to the entire European space, where the ways of circulation retrace more ancient historical and geographical settlement paths. The LC idea of street definitively overpasses the premodern imagery becoming an embryonic figure of what we today recognize as *infrastructure*, combining transport lines to energy ones, long backbones readable at largest scales[7].

«The city has its own precise biology. By its nature it has certain relations in space (the region, the country) and time (past, present, future). The research of routes development leads us to the waterway, to the road, to the railway; the rational route that here we try to identify, will intersect the oldest paths or coincide with them, since history's routes are products of geography.[8]»

Two models for a unique manifesto
«Since the car has overturned the traditional foundations of urbanism, I had conceived the idea of interesting the automobile manufacturers for the setting up of the Esprit Nouveau pavilion at the International Exposition of Decorative Arts, which just had to be devoted to housing and urban planning. "The car has killed the big city. The car must save the big city. Are you willing to study for Paris a Plan Peugeot, Citroen, Voisin of Paris?[9]»

To this unconventional request the only positive response was given by Monsieur Morgemon, administrator of Aéreoplanes G. Voisin (Automobile), who agreed to sponsor the study that then took the name from. The plan, presented in 1925, is the first applied experiment of LC's urban theories formulated in the model for the *Contemporary City*. The abstract grid fits into the existing fabric of the historic center of Paris, in which is articulated the complex of cruciform skyscrapers and redents buildings, standing as the new city center. The integration with the existing fabric is not a strategy compatible with the ambitions of the project, hence the need to act a complete replacement of the old unhealthy quarters for an area along the Seine. Between Place de la Republique and Rue du Louvre and between Gare de l'Est and Rue de Rivoli, as an archaeological excavation on open air, the *Esprit de Paris* lies in few preserved traces. The relationship with the historical structure is solved by LC in an extreme act: on the one hand, eliminating any possibility to refer to the notion of urban tissue replaced by the notion of *block*; on the other, by looking at history in a sense of museological reconciliation between *memory* and *ruin*, leaving the historical traces on the renaturalized ground and dominated by the new artificial and industrious one of the city. The new center is measured by a ground-elevated net of large traffic arteries, organized according to orthogonal directions, distant each others from 50 to 120 meters and crossed transversally every 350 or 400 meters. The new center is linked to a large-scale infrastructural element, a major transport axis of rail and highway, ground- elevated which crosses the city as a new *urbanizing backbone* of Paris.

«And we will add that the road is no longer simply the mainland, but a circulatory apparatus, a new organ, a building that stands on its own, a kind of long factory, which needs one or two floors, and that with a good will, could build cities on pilotis, resorting to a solution of extreme feasibility, achievable when you want.[10]»

The double meaning of infrastructure, as urban frame and as a building organism, is translated in a dual role: as *trace*, it organizes the spatial arrangement of urbanization; as *artifact*, it identifies a basement level through its typological hybridization. The circulatory system allows the extension of the city in the space of its repeatability:

«Breaking the road-corridor, the need is, properly speaking, to create the expansion of the urban landscape. Expansion and not more the single development in depth that is typical of corridor.[11]»

Although devoted to concentration, the city of LC is not dense in its built mass, on the contrary it is disposed in space, in an extended and endless homogeneous way. Transport axes are traced and within these, among these, the urban sectors have been arranged. Through a constant presence of several scales, the infrastructure, in LC intentions, becomes the *binding element* between architecture, urban design and territory. A warping structure which is opposed to the idea of urban form's completeness, and which expands in the open landscape, the elements of the game, setting their variation, their difference as in the case of Algiers experiences. Quoting Tafuri:

«From '29 to '31 with the plans for Montevideo, Buenos Aires, Sao Paulo and Rio and with the final experience of the Plan Obus for Algiers, (...) Le Corbusier breaks the continuous sequence of architecture-blocks-city: the urban structure, both physical and functional, is the trustee of a new scale of values and the dimension to which must be searched the meaning of its communication, is that of the landscape. In Algiers the ancient Kasbah, the hills of Fort l'Empereur, the coastal inlet are assumed as brutes materials to reuse, real ready-made objects on a gigantic scale, to which the new structure that conditions them, offers a unit which did not exist before, overturning its original meanings.[12]»

Although the formal results diverge from the proposal for Paris, *Plan Obus*[13] follows the same design choices that regulate the elements of the urban composition. Indeed it is possible to find similarly the themes of the *ground duplication*, between the new artificial city and that one of the historical and geographical context; the *typological hybridization* between architecture and infrastructure; the *scalar transversality* that crosses the proposal from architecture to territory.

The first sketches for Rio, Montevideo and San Paulo, drawn during his trip to Latin America, present a settlement figure at the geographic scale, strongly indebted to the Roman aqueducts as well as to the European assumptions previously advanced on linear city, which thus become the starting point for the elaboration of an alternative manifesto. In the proposal for the capital of North Africa in 1931, the relation with the ground becomes heavier and the pilotis magnified under the weight of the overlying building of one hundred meters elevation, the viaduct city. It is properly an infrastructure re-conducted to the architectural sign, where the ground level, left free, reveals the wild nature of the place. Within the viaduct system the memory of the preexisting city takes place and is here overtaken by the new artificial plan, conveyed by the circulatory system that dominates the ancient Kasbah. This is still unchanged in its archaeological entirety lying in the shadows of the viaduct, which is projected between the linear city of business, the curved residential redents on the hill of Fort l'Empereur and the civic skyscraper on the downtown port:

«From this point of view, the plan is extended and reinforced. Obus surrounds the Kasbah with tall structures - the skyscraper, the roads, the bridge - from which you can watch below to eternity as a tableau vivant or a postcard. The Kasbah becomes the representation of the other, of a nostalgic other, held in distance.[14]»

The hybridization between infrastructure and urban form becomes the main theme with an almost complete coincidence between trace and artifact. It draws the relations between the different landscape episodes as well as the spatial relationship between architecture and the city. From the urban basement of the proposal for Paris, the *circulation system* in Algiers Plan does not hosts the city in its grid but instead accepts it in the verticality of the linear imprinting, a tape shared by the several urban elements, as in the famous image of the urban roof populated by cars. If, in fact, in the Plan Voisin, infrastructure draws the new artificial ground on which buildings are located, in Plan Obus it redesigns the relationship with the sky, localizing itself with the parking spaces on the upper level and locating the multi-stylish houses below. The unity of the urban section consists of the architectural one, simply rearranging the elements in the precise frame of the LC game's rules.

The collision between geometry and geography
«What Le Corbusier predicted in 1929 came true in many parts, but the fact that the major infrastructures were built with separated logics was fatal to the city and to the landscape they wished to serve. What we treat in this number is however less heroic and unitary. We are rather looking for rules of readjustment, for settlement logics much more empirical and limited, to an attempt of restituting a positive morphological value to the technical intervention, of reasoning on its however ordering role, on the attempt to return it as component of settlement fact.[15]»

The enlargement of the architectural discipline to the semantic sphere of the territory finds a specific cultural background in the Italian research on the *Grande Dimensione*, involving the general panorama of the architectural discipline in the sixties and seventies, represented by some important figures such as Giuseppe Samonà, Ludovico Quaroni, Ernesto Nathan Rogers. In its formative period Vittorio Gregotti crosses, indeed, two main theoretic paths: the *unity between architecture and urban planning* promulgated by Samonà[16] while he was director of the IUAV venice where Gregotti himself started his academic career, and the notion of *environmental pre-existences* promulgated by Rogers through the Casabella magazine[17]. The *school of reality* and the abandonment of utopia are the two premises of profound theoretical revision made by Gregotti since the Triennale of Milano in 1964. The motto *Restart from the territory*, as an anthropogeographic palimpsest and actor of an interdisciplinary dialogue, is the main theoretical assumption underlying a renewed emphasis on infrastructure.

«It is possible to build a new notion of physical environment linked to the very essence of architecture. This environment must be considered a kind of real continuum available to be organized according to goals that can be defined as the expansion of the possibility of using the environment itself.[18]»

Gregotti's critical position was first developed in the book *The Territory of Architecture* and later through the *Casabella Editorials*, under his leadership from 1982 to 1996. The relationship between architecture and infrastructure once again becomes crucial. Architecture, such as infrastructure, indeed, acquires significance as expression of a concrete settlement act, transcending its objectual dimension, disregarding its own linguistic and formal internal code and pouring it in the matter of the territory. Quoting Gregotti architecture is «construction of a conscious geography that is offered as a meaningful image of the environment in which we move», and at the same time as a model which corresponds the need of *figure*[19]. In this sense, architecture consists of a figurative quality in the wider semantic framework of infrastructure, which invests necessarily the role of foundation, similar to that of tracing a road and of disposing relations. This disciplinary cross-border between two worlds becomes the *fil rouge* that underlies the subsequent theoretical elaborations and experimental design proposals of the seventies, in which Gregotti from time to time explores and explains characters and operational tools for the project. The first tool is given by the *settlement principle* that combines both architectural and infrastructural signs. It is intended as an act of rational measurement by which the project and the context are placed in a dialoguing condition. The essential difference, indeed, with respect to the Le Corbusier disposal of the infrastructural city is given by the fact that the settlement model has an *architectural nature*, as finite and not repeatable morphology, where the relationship between parts is measured with exact precision:

«A conception so dynamic of the project must refer to an idea of architecture not as isolated artifact but as a system of relationships, of intervals between things. Not the idea of a space as an uniform and infinite extension, but of the specificity, the difference, the discontinuity as a value, then, of the idea of place as geography and history, and of the settlement principle as an act of evidence of that place by means of architecture.[20]»

The interscalarity of Gregotti territorial projects fit into a precise balance between clarity of the settlement choices and spatial values. A combination that highlights the ambiguity of the linguistic code adopted in many projects, where Gregotti explores the spatiality of *bridge-building, dam-building, centuriation building* combining technological and structural principles belonging to Transport Engineering and reinstalling them within the research field of architecture and spatial design. The elements that Gregotti uses, similarly to LC, are quantitatively and typologically limited, an alphabet continuously reshaped. In this procedure, the technique of *paratactic montage* is evident both at the scale of the landscape, where different materials and bodies, both at the scale of building construction in which the elements of the composition are no longer merged as in LC sections, but juxtaposed in their independence.

The project for the Università delle Calabrie
«How to dominate with the morphological tools of architecture the geographical scale, (...), the project of the University of Calabria is also an attempt to investigate the possibility of identifying these instruments for the control and the recognition of a territorial identity, to measure the planimetric vision and the elevation, and to give unity in large complex systems.[21]»

The project for the *Università delle Calabrie*, as winning entry of the Ideas Competition in 1973[22], was implemented and realized in more than twenty years. It has important precedents as the *Amalassunta* project (1971), the Samonà design proposal for the *Università di Cagliari* (1972), or the project for the *Asse Attrezzato in Latina* of Purini/Thermes (1968). These examples, among others, although with different formal results are based on the incorporation of settlement principles in the unity of the architectural vision. As in the case of the Università delle Calabrie, they refer to *infrastructural architectures*.

The Arcavacata Campus, in Calabria region, is articulated starting from the geometric grid of 25,20 x 25,20 meters, which is the measure of the departments symmetrically arranged along the two-levels bridge axis, equipped for vehicular and pedestrian traffic. The plan is disposed on a constant buiding elevation quote of 243.40 meters above sea level. As a landmark due to the constant line of the bridge, it projects the new intervention into the landscape, for a length, in the original design proposal, of more than 3 km. This tightrope slopes on Arcavacata hills and connects, in the intentions of the architect, different infrastructural lines: on the north the Salerno-Reggio Calabria highway and the provincial road of the Silana-Crotonese, on the south the railway line that links the city to the national railroad on the Tyrrhenian coast. The settlement model, with the arrangement of the north-south axis, constitutes at the same time a *trace d'union* between the several infrastructural lines, and a cultural infrastructure for the area in its ideal reference to a "bridge-building".

The project assumes in itself the landscape identity as a strategic element in the overlapping of a new artificial geography, able to measure the natural scene in a unitary design on a large scale and reconciling two morphological systems. The first one, geometric, is given by the linear sequence of departments blocks that measure the variability of gradients through the constant height of the deck of the bridge; the second one, natural, is given by the system of the sinuous hills which intercept the project in the graft of public open spaces, squares, such as pedestrian and vehicular connections with the existing road network. Another element of the collision between the strict geometry of the infrastructural sign and the accidental nature of the site is given by the design of the ground level, in which the spaces change favoring the hill's section. In this counterpoint the ground is an inhabited common space, strongly characterized through spatial sequences juxtaposed and differentiated.

Two other characters are of great interest: the *ambiguity* of the linguistic code and the *typological hybridization*. In this case, indeed, is clear a typological invention given by the combination of the the buildings that constitute the transversal section of the complex -the departments block, the equipped bridge, the ground level- which, however, do not find a proper unit. Indeed while in the structure of Plan Obus the viaduct/building is described as an organic whole creating a unique architecture, in the Arcavacata project the elements remain formally and spatially distincted, juxtaposed in a compositional montage[23]. In this approach is staged the dissonance between the extension of the landscape and this *finite machine* to which is dialogically opposed opposed. The architect enlightens the disposition of a spatial architectural set related to a specific context, where the built form recaptures a strict dialogue with the landscape, in which the general order is identified in the blurred line between architecture and territorial infrastructure. The dispositive of the University appears as the concretion of possible relations between architecture, landscape and infrastructure.

«The ambition to achieve an architecture made of pure relations seems here satisfied: what remains of the object, does not live in the natural environment, it is rather "confused", feeling forced to huddle close behind the only reference in that environment is welcomed as solidified eco of a word always pronounced by the choir of the hills and valleys: the secure and indifferent line that overrides every natural accident and gets the strength of its consisting of pure sign.[24]»

Architectural singularity and infrastructural iperurbanity
«What we're interested in, is the development of new models, as a result of urban experiences of the eighties and nineties, we should now focus on discovery of a new type of city planning that is opposed to the idea of the city as a ordered set of objects and we should promote forms rarely expressed that have no architectural relationship with each other.[25]»

The critical position of Rem Koolhaas on the construction of the contemporary city grounds on the assumption of independence of architectural form respect to the context, and consequently on the impossibility of creating a coordinated urban system between parts. This radical position can be firstly referred to some competition experiences of the seventies and eighties. In particular the one at the Berlin Sommerakademie in 1977 where, as member of the design team constituted around O.M. Ungers, develops the project *The City within the City, Berlin as a green archipelago*[26]. The awareness of a crisis in the future demographic projections for Berlin coincides with the proposal of its deconstruction. The void replaces the building fabric, entrusting the urban image to few remarkable places in which densifying collective memory and symbolic meaning. The main thesis of the proposal grounds on the recognition of this new urban morphology built on voids, reducing the urban tissues to singular fragments. As islands of identity, they constitute semantic units immersed in a green and uninhabited vacuum where infrastructures and recreational common spaces are located. Even if concluded in their architectural configuration, they seem to have lost any relationship with the context along with the ability to intervene, change or be changed from the outside. A new monumentality that lessens fragments of urban form to *iconic landmarks*, as if the significance of the construction of city could be condensed in some intelligible representations. The Berlin experience is a prerequisite to the theoretical work on the city for the Dutch architect that no longer recognizes, within the contemporary condition, the possibility of a relational structure able to weave the threads of the metropolitan development, role entrusted in the previous readings by the infrastructural system. There are two complementary themes on which Koolhaas focuses about the future visions of the city: the need to think *the void as design space*, as the only possible restitution of a collective meaning compared to a built mass become uncontrollable, and the *reduction of the urban image to isolated elements*. Koolhaas entrusts the hypothesis of *formal independence of architectural objects* as a new morphogenetic root, generative of an *iperurban condition*. The spatial densification becomes, indeed, a constant theme developed through functional hybridization, design layer's proliferation and continuous juxtaposition of heterogeneous worlds to *mimic* the crowded contemporary urban horizon. Densification and iperurbanity characterize the idea of an architectural object that, just in its scalar gigantism, opens up to a size between architectural and urban design able to frame the city scene itself.

The design *of OMA, Koolhaas and Mau in 1995* for the new town of Melun-Senart *(OMA, Koolhaas and Mau, 1995)* takes up the theme of the void as main figure to work on the construction of the new urban center, which is identified as a field of pure potentiality, imagining «the quality of nowhere, at the heart of the metropolis». The attack that Koolhaas addresses to contemporary european city is, in fact, to live through a mask of stability of its image that does not really longer corresponds to its true contemporary essence, made of an indistinct magma. As pure potential it allows to attract and receive the different lines of force transforming constantly its polymorphic condition:

«In a model of urban metropolitan solids and voids, the desire for stability and the needs of the unstable are not incompatible. They can be carried out as two separate entities, connected by invisible connections. Through the parallel action of reconstruction and destruction, a city can become an archipelago of architectural islands floating in a post-architectural landscape or deleted, where what was used to be city is densely replaced by a significant anything. The type of consistency that can reach the metropolis is not that of a composition homogeneously planned. Can be, at most, a system of fragments, a system of multiple realities; in Europe, the remainder of the historical heart may belong to this system.[27]»

Parallel to the formulation of a vision on the extreme contemporary urban condition, Koolhaas and OMA address more specifically the relationship between infrastructure and urban form through the projects of *Zeebrugge Sea Terminal* and *Euralille*, both of 1989, and the *Center for Transportation Exchange in Benelux* of 1991. In all the three projects, which deal with the issue of infrastructural accessibility, the team grounds the initial hypothesis of a contemporary culture of congestion, previously highlighted and represented by the Manhattan model[28]. Congestion is combined with architectural gigantism, declaring the role of architecture as spatial urban condenser, node of modal interchange, which retains its own figure in an objectual un-finitude of the building.

«If there must be a new urbanism it will not be based on the twins fantasies of order and omnipotence, will be the staging of uncertainty, will not have to do with the dislocation of objects more or less permanent but with the potential irradiation in the territories; do not aspire to stable configurations but of fields actions to locate processes that refuse to be crystallized in final form, will no longer be meticulous definition, imposition of limits, but expansion of notions, cancellation of margins, failure to identify entities, but the discovery of unspeakable hybrids, no longer obsessed with the idea of the city but by the manipulation of infrastructure for intensification and endless diversifications, shortcuts and redistribution, the reinvention of psychological space.[29]»

Architecture, as point of reference of an extended sense of place, renounces its specificity and identity, to become uncomplete landmarks. This spatial proliferation, in a continuous overlapping of virtual and physical places simultaneously present in the same scene, according to the Dutch architect, is an essential feature of contemporary, a character necessarily evoked, explored and made explicit in the new internity of public space and in the encompassment of infrastructure within the architectural object.

«Why do not conceive vast bastard cities: gigantic architectural accumulations, huge-buffer buildings, urban outposts beyond the idea of the city, urban obstacles that simply absorb all flows, swallow things, cars, people from any part they arrive? Suddenly the highways could end in them; they could be used to easily park, take trains, trams, buses, or be any witness to a collective moment, towards the center - transfer from anywhere to anywhere.[30]»

Buildings, argues the architect, who in their authentic brutality could save the sense of civilization as we know it.

Euralille, a dislocated city
In the experience for Lille, the design issue of the emptyness and the role of architecture as a condensed iperurbanity seem to be wrapped around the presence of infrastructure. Conceived at the end of the eighties, Euralille represents the symbol of a reunified Europe, that gives rise to the future vision of the city as the nerve center of transport intersection. The two necessary conditions for its repositioning within the logic of transnational exchanges are identified in the construction of the Tunnel which connects London to Paris and the accelerated extension of the high-speed railway lines in France:

«a center of European interest, a place capable of delivering regeneration of tertiary activities of the metropolis of Lille and the French region of the North Pas-De-Calais, to reposition the city and the metropolitan area that it would result in the levels of competitiveness with the major metropolitan European configurations.[31]»

The same ambition is implemented by Koolhaas, unanimously selected as winning competition entry team within an international consultation launched in September 1988[32], affirming the absolute positional value of the project within a European territorial macroscale:

«If this hypothesis comes true, the city of Lille, the center of gravity of the triangle London-Brussels-Paris, suddenly will take a theoretical importance, becoming a receptacle for a large number of typical activities of the modern age. In the contemporary world, the programs become abstraction in the sense that they are not more specifically related to a specific context or city: they gravitate and fluctuate in an opportunistic way around the places that offer more connections.[33]»

Euralille represents a new model, the vision of a *dislocated city*, which doesn't refers exclusively to a specific location or con-

Manifesti   **57**

text, but to a symbolic condition of contemporary dwelling, surrounded by a system of nodes and networks that claim another level of understanding, represented through the architectural scalar gigantism of the building program. The project itself is finalized to envision thus a new model for urbanization that represent the emergent character of the western Europe.

«Euralille configures itself as the construction of a project within a city - in other words is not an extension of this city, it does not belong completely to that but rather constitutes a part of a more widespread system that connects London to Eurodisney. And so the question is how to integrate a process of inevitable modernization for Europe, and that will completely transform, within countries and cities that already exist? (...) Euralille is both in Lille both depends on this without destroying it in any way, without creating any form of aggregation.[34]»

In this transnational geography the individual is citizen of a unique European metro network in which the stops constitute the iperurban centers of condensation, where the future business meets at infrastructural intersections, rather than in the city cores. The innovation of the project is revealed in the program with an attempt to represent this new urban reality of the future European city:

«No doubt EuraLille is, by Koolhaas, not far as the citadel, a "wedge" stacked in the urban fault that has its own autonomy. It is an International addition that should not be sweetened with the local value, which adapts itself to certain points of the territory and whose architectural breaking is in the logic of program.[35]»

The erasing of both notions of urban tissue and of modernist block, contributes in defining the project for the International Center as a structure held together by fragments whose dialogue does not happen anymore on a urban scale, in the construction of the scene, but on the architectural one relating different pieces to a functional and iconic unity. The infrastructure and its representation become required keys for reading the place, in the purpose of an expressive extremization. The site which is located the new project for a Business City consists of an irregular band of infrastructural residual areas, riding a network of transportation lines, and at the same time a transition between the urban center and its first peripheral expansion. It extends for a length of two kilometers adjacent to the ancient wall and the Green Circle, a green belt that still represents a liminal void between the historical center and the more recent expansions.

The complexity of the site, as well as that of the program characterize this theoretical manifesto: spatial density and intensity of experience are the main pillars for the project development articulated around architectural singularities and displacements. The program to be conveyed in the area presents an over-concentration of public and tertiary functions: exhibitions and conference centers, trade fair spaces, shopping malls, accommodation services such as hotels and dormitories for students, urban park, theater, office towers. Within a general articulation the whole, therefore, reveals itself as a complex system made up of autonomous differences, parts that conflict with respect to the infrastructural bundles more than engaging a conscious paradigm of contemporary metropolitan status. Precisely in this regard Koolhaas focuses on the configuration of the intermodal station and parking area that is no longer considered as a building entity but as an *infrastructural plinth*, a basement in which the vectors of communication and transport hover in a *Piranesian space*. This definition represents a generative morphological root very present in the current infrastructural transformations, that sees the infrastructure not taking its own formal connotation, as it was in the Modern Architecture, but becoming progressively an interior space, embodying the essential condition of a contemporary nomadism.

Expression, therefore, of the metropolitan physical groundless, of an *immaterial congestive culture*. Finally, another character of the project concerning the relation infrastructure/architecture, is the neutrality of the linguistic code adopted by Koolhaas that, contrary to the strong tendency of structural expressiveness of the two previous readings, it vanishes in the will of an unscalar intervention and further disorientation given by a non-structural, formal and metric spaces. To this linguistic neutrality refers the diagrammatic character of architecture that replaces the program to the form:

«in explaining the projects, OMAMO punctualize the fact that on this organizational scale, architecture identifies itself with the urban sphere and, "the building is an infrastructure that organizes the presence of different elements. A diagram of its organization more echoes in the maps of the underground lines than in architectural plans". In addition, the organizational diagram in question is a diagrammatic section. In other words, there is a double slip: a leap in scale - from architecture to urban - and a change of position, rotating the horizontal plan in the vertical one.[36]»

1. Le Corbusier (1923) *Urbanisme*. Gallimard, Paris. Ed.it (1967). *Urbanistica*. Il Saggiatore, Milano, p. 91.

2. The interrelation between urban form and infrastructure becomes a constant in LC work on the city, from 1924 with *Urbanisme* to 1946 with *Manière de penser l'urbanisme*, for more than twenty years of publications at the turn of the two wars.

3. Le Corbusier (ed. it 1967). *Op. cit*, p. 168.

4. *Ibidem*, p. 168.

5. With the pedestrian flow on the ground and the mechanical on the elevated one, are also analyzed, in the same volume, the different kind of interrelation between the street and the external context, open landscape or urban fabric. The functional hierarchy of the street is later stigmatized in the Theory of 7V, which has in Chandigarh the most clear experimental application.

6. «Le Corbusier's architectural vocabulary is defined and established from the beginning, even though it becomes richer and transforms itself over time. The new elements, when there are any, are not the ones that characterize and give content to the successive urban models; instead, this role is played by the relations established between these elements. Soon, Le Corbusier understood that to develop the forms of the composition in an endless way, in any discipline, it was sufficient to provide oneself with an alphabet made of a restricted number of signs.» Aris, M.C. (2010) Bogotà: aerial view. In AA.VV (ed.). *LCBOG. Le Corbusier en Bogotà 1947-1951*. Ediciones Uniandes, Bogota.

7. See the *Euromediterranen Project*. Le Corbusier, (1946) *Manière de penser l'urbanisme*. Ed. It. (1965). *Maniera di pensare l'urbanistica*. Laterza Editore, Roma, p.125.

8. *Ibidem*, p. 103.

9. Le Corbusier (ed. it 1967). *Op. cit*, p. 92.

10. *Ibidem*, p.123.

11. *Ibidem*, p.93.

12. Tafuri, M.(1973) *Progetto e utopia*. Laterza Editore, Bari, p.216.

13. Referred to Project A, 1931-1934. In Le Corbusier, (1935). *La Ville Radieuse*. Editions Vincent, Paris.

14. Lipstadt, H; Mendelsohn, H. (1993) Philosophy, History and Autobiography: Manfredo Tafuri and the "Unsurpassed Lesson" of Le Corbusier. *Assemblage*, n°22, pp. 58-103.

15. Gregotti, V. (1989) La strada, tracciato e manufatto. *Casabella*, n° 553-554.

16. Samonà, G. (1964). *La città territorio*. Bari: De Donato Editore

17. Rogers, E.N. (1968). *Editoriali di architettura*. Torino: Einaudi

18. Gregotti, V. (1965). Relazione al Convegno INU Trieste. In Gregotti, V. (1979) *Il progetto per l'Università delle Calabrie e altre architetture*. Electa, Milano.

19. Gregotti, V. (1967) *Il Territorio dell'Architettura*. Feltrinelli, Bologna, p.80.

20. Gregotti, V. (1970) Introduzione al corso di Composizione Architettonica, Palermo. In Gregotti, V. (1979). *Op.cit*.

21. *Ibidem*, p. 76.

22. The competition team for the project was composed by V. Gregotti (team leader), E. Battisti, H. Matsui, P. Nicolin, F. Purini, C. Rusconi Clerici, B. Viganò.

23. Purini, F. (2013). *Sette tipi di semplicità in architettura*. Melfi: Libria.

24. Tafuri, M. (1979). Le avventure dell'oggetto: architetture e progetti di Vittorio Gregotti. In Gregotti, V. (1979). *Op.cit*.

25. Zaera Polo, A. (1992) Finding Freedoms. Conversations with Rem Koolhaas. *El Croquis*, n°53.

26. The project team was composed by O.M. Ungers (team leader), H. Kollhoff and R. Koolhaas.

27. Koolhaas, R. (1985) Imagining the Nothingness. In OMA; Koolhaas, R.; Mau, B. (1995). *Op. cit*., p. 198.

28. Koolhaas, R. (1978). *Delirious New York, A retroactive manifesto for Manhattan*. New York: The Monacelli Press.

29. Koolhaas, R. (1995) Whatever happened to Urbanism. In OMA; Koolhaas, R.; Mau, B. (1995). *Op. cit*., p. 969.

30. Koolhaas, R. (1991) Dolphins. Transportation Center for Benelux. In OMA; Koolhaas, R.; Mau, B. (1995). *Op. cit*. p. 999.

31. Baïetto, J.P. (1988). *Euralille Métropole. Premières étapes de definition du projet*. Euralille archives, Lille.

32. To the Euralille competition were invited eight offices represented by: Claude Vasconi, Jean-Paul Viguier, Yves Lion, e Michel Macary; Norman Foster, Vittorio Gregotti, Oswald Mathias Ungers, e Rem Koolhaas.

33. Koolhaas, R. (1995) Un salto quantistico. *Casabella*, n°623.

34. Menu, I.; Vermandel, F. (1996) Interview with Rem Koolhaas. In Koolhaas, R.; Nouvel, J.; Portzamparc, C.; Vasconi, C.; Duihueill (ed) *Euralille. The making of a new city*. Birkhauser, Berlin, p. 51.

350. Treiber, D. (1995) OMA a Euralille: una angosciata modernità. *Casabella*, n° 623.

36. Cortès, J. A. (2006) Delirious and more. II Strategy vs Architecture. *El Croquis*, n°131/132.

3.3

3. Zuidas, Southern Axis Amsterdam (2000/ 2033)

Masterplan design: City of Amsterdam Physical Planning Department (DRO); Arup London

The masterplan is focused on the construction of a large stacked tunnel where will pass the infrastructural lines -highway, railway and high speed - giving the possibility to build up a new ground where will grow up an high density urban district, filling the area through a series of tertiary towers.

Images credits
3.1 Amsterdam Zuidas
source: Franklin Heijnen, (flickr, CC)

3.2 Zuidas Business District @ Amsterdam
source: Guilhem Vellut, (flickr, CC)

3.3 Zuidas Amsterdam
source: Arden, (flickr, CC)

4. Hafen City, New Inner City District. Hamburg (2000/2025)

Masterplan design: Kees Christiaanse / ASTOC (Masterplan)

Hafen City is one of the biggest and most important urban redevelopment project of harbor area at European level. The opportunity for Hamburg was represented by the disposal of the ancient trading port, moved to a wider area in the south-east, which freed the river front from industrial activities.

Images credits
4.1 View towards Hafen City, Hamburg
source: Rob Deutscher, (flickr, CC)

4.2 Luftbild: Elbphilharmnonie in Hamburg
source: Marco Verch, (flickr, CC)

4.1

4.2

5. Oresund Rhegion, Copenhagen-Malmo (1995/2000 bridge construction)

The priority project n.11, of the TEN-T program, ie the Stable link of the bridge/tunnel between Copenhagen and Malmo, completed in 2000, puts in place a series of urban projects of major importance, which are carrying out a profound transformation in the urban dynamics of the two cities, increasing their competitiveness on a regional scale. In Copenhagen with the ongoing realization of a new urban district (Ørestad) and in Malmo with the complete renovation of the old port (Västra Hamnen).

Images credits
Øresund bridge
source: Johan Wessman;
© News Øresund (CC BY 3.0)

6. Berlin Central Station (1992/2006)

Masterplan design: Gerkan, Marg e Partner (gmp) HAmburg

Images credits
Berliner Hauptbahnhof
source: Sascha Kohlmann, (flickr, CC)

7. Liege - Guillelmins Central Station (1992/2006)

Masterplan design: Santiago Calatrava Architects

Images credits
Gare de Liège-Guillemins
source: Marcus Pink,(flickr, CC)

Contemporary morphotypes

A conflicting relation. Infrastructural morphotypes & the contemporary urban scene of the European Metropolis

In last decades territories have been affected by constant physical mutations due to the increment of infrastructural backbones, coagulating around and along them new forms of dwelling, whose thrust takes consistency from a specific *condition of reciprocity*. However, contrary to the understanding of this phenomenon as strictly related and circumscribed to the contemporary condition of a globalized world, the arguments exposed in the previous chapter of this contribution, pose a fundamental interpretation of the today relationship between infrastructure and urban form. Largely described as dusty system or infinite city, the thesis argues that this phenomenon is not, a contemporary product of the ever changing society but actually the ultimate consequence of a deep split of urban scene's unity right occurred in Modernism. Far away from its original meaning of simple connecting line[1] between two entities, infrastructure conquers, at the beginning of the XXth century, a proper role in urban researches as new form equal to the status of built fabric within the construction of the industrial city. Two opposite positions highlight the dilemma of this *semantic overturn*[2]. From one side the thesis on the unity of urban scene by Camillo Sitte:

«It is due to the fact, easily observable, that in all the ancient squares the roads flow into one space, on the contrary to that practiced by today's builders of the city. Today it has become the current rule to converge at each corner of the square two roads that cut perpendicularly, which has the consequence that the opening towards the square is enlarged and the overall effect is greatly impaired, if not destroyed.»[3]

While opposite is the position of Le Corbusier:

«Urbanism will abandon the current street-corridor, and through the path of new developments will create, on a much larger scale, the architectural symphony that need to be conducted. The street-corridor with two sidewalks, suffocated by high houses, must disappear. Cities have the right to be something else that many buildings with corridors.»[4]

Modernism recognizes infrastructure as a physical and autonomous element that weaves precise material relationships within the context. Its meaning is characterized by a disciplinary cross-border that refers to an implicit continuity of its role between the morphological dimension of architecture and the ordering one of spatial planning. The first considers infrastructure as an *artifact* that involves the sphere of design through a formal category, while the second of planning considers infrastructure as the *ordering principle* of settlement. Actually the affirmation of this double meaning - especially along the Second Modernism - deeply influenced architectural research and design approaches, pushing results to interpret infrastructure as inhabiting space. It is a fact that along the second phase of Modernism, after the second world war, the attention of several researches was pointed on a design process of hybridization of infrastructural spaces, as clearly outlined by Robert Venturi in his important essay *Complexity and Contradiction in Architecture*:

«To the Algeri project that is housing and highway, and to the last projects of Wright for Pittsburg Point and for Bagdad respond "le viaduct architecture" of Kahn and the "collective form" of Fumiko Maki. Such architectures incorporate into a unitary whole complex and contradictory hierarchies of scale and movement, structure and space. They are buildings and bridges at the same time. And switching to a larger scale: a dam is both a bridge, the Chicago Loop is both a border and a circulation system, and the Kahn road wants to be a building (...) valid ambiguity arises useful flexibility.»[5]

However, if modern infrastructural archetypes, as railway galleries and automobile corridors, represented autonomous entities embodying distinct figures and strictly codified typologies, today's infrastructural interventions exceed their original figurativeness by new configurations that show a massive enlargement of spatial dimensions and functional complexity. The leading approaches, indeed, are not struggling on the translation onto forms of specific transport modes -i.e. railways, highway, ports or airports-, they don't differ the ones from the others. On the contrary the strategy of hybridization, with the aim to combine the logistic functional needs -transport systems- and the aspirations of grounding the inhabiting values of infrastructures -social and economic trends of mobility-, gradually have been dissolving infrastructural typology solutions into a morphological discourse. Infrastructural strategies are now firstly dealing with their contextualized position in urban or territorial conditions, and with the attempt to enhance the intersection of diverse flows and scales. Indeed, the principal design strategies can be outlined through specific *modalities of engagement* between infrastructure and urban body. Engagement that is expressed, more and more often, through a *figurative irreconcilability* between the two, where the infrastructure, exponentially loaded, over time has become progressively a factor of social exclusion, of physical break and, for this reason, of conflict within the social scene.
Through a critical reading of the on going and recent projects in European metropolis, three main modalities of engagement between infrastructure and urban form can be identified. Huge infrastructural basements unfold and redraw entire parts of city underground, suggesting unique and reassuring images of a

controllable urbanity reconstructed as a *simulacrum* within the complex, pervasive and enveloping transport network system. Examples are the new intermodal transport models like the *Barajas Airport* in Madrid or the *Berlin-Brandenburg*, with the attempt to declare their urban values onto the architectural scale of infrastructure. Instead of representing a proper spatial identity regarding the idea and the meanings of contemporary mobility, they seem to reach an alternative urbanity, in a sort of *semantic duplication*. The progressive disappearing of infrastructure declines itself also through the phenomenon of *substitution*. While in the first modality the attempt is to relocate infrastructures in underground areas, the second one tends towards their complete replacement with new fragments of urbanity, as for example the case of *HafenCity*[6] in Hamburg or the redevelopment of the port areas in Helsinki[7]. In these proposals is peculiar the act of replacing the infrastructural presence with new residential or mixed areas, completely erasing traces and memories of more gray and smoky remains of a Modern past. But is it about refusing history, removing a trauma from urban memory? Or is it nowadays possible to think, for the European context, in terms of simply considering the contruction of urban form as a substituve sequence of scenic courtains? On the opposite side is present the on going process of *densification* around and near the infrastructural nodes, that express the third modality of engagement, following the *Euralille* model as clear hybridization manifesto of the eighties[8]. The plans for *Zuidas* in Amsterdam or for *Rotterdam Central Station* show that, by returning infrastructural tracks on the underground, it is possible to reconvert residual areas in high-density districts, often emerging as antagonist centralities to the consolidated urban nucleus. Nowadays these huge transformations are a primary mean of financial attractiveness as privileged sites for new demographic and labor flows and engines of economic development.

All the three identified modalities of engagement -duplication, substitution, densification- are characterized by a sort of figurative irreconcilability, evident in the fact that the one's presence excludes the other and viceversa. In this conflicting relation the 'aut/aut' condition generates diverse figures, that can be more properly explained as *infrastructural morphotypes*, emerging in the today urban portrait and able to weave upcoming scenarios, as bearers of innovation, readdressing both critical reading instruments and design methods. With the term of *morphotype* is primarily intended the acquired complexity of these interventions that cannot be described or limited to codified infrastructural typologies, but on the contrary -due to the development of a long process of spatial hybridization-, they present themselves as constituted by the combination and the co-presence of several parts. This co-presence can be traced as constant in all the interventions.

Moreover *morphotype*[9] means also the strong influence that external conditions - i.e. the urban context - execute on the overall system configuration. Context and scale are, in this perspective, fundamental features of infrastructural projects, in which their re-signification aims:

«to shift the focus to the structural characteristics of the context, researching a formal structure of larger geographical areas, in which the architectural phenomenon expresses its own identity through a system of recurring relations.[10]»

The main common characters of infrastructural morphotypes consist, indeed, in the fact that they work for assembly and merging of different building types and functional complexity, grounding their articulation depending on the specificity of site and context, so that they just can be understood through the drawing instrument of the *section*. Analyzing its strata, from the bottom to the top, different layers construct the thick section of infrastructural junctions. From urban flows, represented by metro lines, tubes connect the diverse layers of mobility, from local to larger networks consisting of railways tunnels laying under the ground space of the city, the public realm. The space of connection within the underground mobility plinths is mostly represented by interior semi-public promenades often accompanied by services and commercial hubs. Finally out from the infrastructural womb, a new skyline is composed by business centers, tertiary towers for offices and services as well as residential buildings and hotels. Within this ideal section are identified three main morphotypes that, depending on their positional value within the city, differ each other's not because of their components but mostly for the figurative results and thickness. Namely the identified figures are presented as *the divided ground*, *the basement* and *the platform*.

The Divided Ground
The first figure of infrastructural morphotypes concerns the relation between infrastructure and the re-appropriation of nature within urban and territorial contexts. It regards mainly linear intervention or bypasses, placed in the hinge areas where infrastructure has been historically considered a gap between city's parts. The leitmotiv of the ground reconfiguration through green or blue infrastructure, as for example the *Madrid Rio project*[11], is based on the ecological reconstruction through the presence of nature within the city. The place of the conflict is now conquered by an 'artificial ecology', which redraws the cities' ground and internalizes infrastructural figurativeness. In general terms, this trend allows to trace an emerging twenty-first century iconography that evokes a new arcadia for future scenarios, solving this conflicting relation in the *disappearance of infrastructure from urban scene*. The doubled ground doesn't generate any exchange between the pattern of mobility and the urban form. A clear example of that is given by the project *Avenue2 De Groene Loper*[12] in Maastricht. The construction of a stacked two layer tunnel that runs below the urban belt, for a length of 2.3 kilometers, will replace the fast lanes of highways with a cycle-pedestrian promenade, the green ribbon, delimited by trees and roads for the local traffic flows.

The project involves, with the completion of the new underground infrastructure, the renovation of several areas along the route. A new urban scene made by residential buildings, will be also redesigned at the entrances of the underground highway, Europaplein and Geusselt areas, where buildings complex will reshape the north and south gateways of the hidden infrastructural line. On the east side is currently under construction a new neighbourhood near the stadium with the implementation of sports and leisure activities and services. The proposal of a new ground appears as an 'infrastructural camouflage'[13], with the creation of a recreational park of more than 2000 trees standing on a completely artificial basement, reversing the public imagery of the now expanded urban centre.

The Basement
The second category does not relate to the cases of linear infrastructures but to that one of nodes, where the thickness of spatial dimension widens to assume a dimension of urban plinth, reproducing in its interior a public city scenography. Even in this case the strategy of an urban needle follows the construction of an underground infrastructure, that never matches with the urban ground. Progressively enlarging the dimensions of the underground spaces, these interventions mostly refer to intermodal nodes located in the metropolitan areas cores, representing crucial point that matches different mobility layers. It is the case, for example, of the *Parque Central*[14] in Valencia. The redevelopment of the railway area, a real historical caesura in the city heart, is based on a new underground tunnel arriving to the Central Station, because of the high speed line construction. The general plan signs some focal points along the reconstruction of the avenida that will connect the south zone to the central urban area. Along the new axis is located a linear green park that converges in the area of the Parque Central, an existing rail yard, that will be the first city green lung. Furthermore, the road axis generates a deep renovation action for the residual lots on its boundaries. New plots

are implanted on the existing urban grid, in which are disposed the residential and mixed use buildings. Their layout as well as the relation between voids and solids follows a rationalist composition. High buildings - tertiary towers - are located at the new park's entrances as visual landmarks of the city skyline.

The Platform
A third figure of the irreconciliability between urban form and infrastructure is envisioned in the concept of the platform, where the infrastructural density appears at the city limits. Indeed these interventions occur in a greater need of surface able to host a dense field of lines, traces, viaducts and building voted to mobility. Patterns that take up more and more impressive bands of liminal territory, becoming no more doors as stations were for the modern city, but real infrastructural thresholds, whereas the increasing extensions fall within a more complex imagery. As in the second figure, also in this case emerge a strictly codified typology related to the embodiment of mobility and transnational society iconography through the type of high-rise buildings and business centres. They constitute new typological hybridizations between infrastructure, settlements' principles and public realm. The project for the Amsterdam Southern Axis has its origins in the *Plan Zuid* of H.P. Berlage presented in 1914. However the effective development of the expansion plan started at the end of the nineties, when the municipality promoted a new strategic role, for the entire area: a gateway for trade and transport related to international traffic flows[15]. The masterplan focuses on the construction of a large and stacked tunnel that hosts the infrastructural traces -highway, railway and high speed lines - giving the possibility to build a new ground where an high density urban district grows up, filling the area through a series of tertiary towers. The completion of the entire work, expected in 2030, is implemented through different temporal phases of construction and divided into three main areas of high density program - West, Centre, East -. The entire district, once completed, will assume a great

importance as international hub, thanks to the presence of an articulated and complex network of transport system.

Over a certain scale and complexity several infrastructural and urban projects underwent to big crisis during the realization phase, crisis, both due to the historical economic moment of the last decade and to the high level costs imposed on the context. A closed circuit that implicate great economic involvement with low impact in social environment. In addition to an unequal balance, the interventions appear conceptually outdated already in their beginnings: highly indebted towards the infrastructural imagery of Modernism and less experimental with regard to the emerging transport technologies.

8.1

8.2

Intersections and ambiguity

8. Madrid Rìo (2003/2008)

Masterplan design: West 8; MRIO (Burgos & Garrido, Porras La Casta e Rubio Álvarez-Sala)

The Madrid Rìo is a park born from the provision through which, between 2003 and 2007, the city administration interrupted a stretch of the M-30, an artery of the city ring road built in the '70 parallel to the river Manzanares.

Images credits
8.1 Riverside promenade, Madrid
source: La Citta Vita (flickr, CC)

8.2 Madrid Río
source: Relampague (flickr, CC)

---

9. Porta Susa Central Station Torino (2002/2013)

Masterplan design: Silvio D'Ascia Architectures

Images credits
9.1 Porta Susa station, Turin, Italy
source: MaxDeVa (flickr, CC)

9.2 Porta Susa
source: Stefano Costa (flickr, CC)

---

10. Utrecht Central Station Leidsche Rijn (2008/2016-2025)

Masterplan station design: Benthem Crouwel Architekten
Masterplan urban design: JCAU Architects

Images credits
Station Utrecht Centraal
source: Rob Dammers,(flickr, CC)

---

11. Wien New Central Station, Central Brownfield Development. Wien (2006/2015)

Masterplan design: A. Wimmer, E. Hofmann, T. Hotz architects

The redevelopment of the Railway South Area is an ambitious program of upgrading not only for the new station's contruction - an intermodal hub and crossing node for Trans European networks -, but also for Wien's urban fabric. The area involved in the project is about 109 hectares and will host a new mixed-use urban district that will define, with the group of tertiary towers, the contemporary city iconography.

Images credits
Wien Hbf
source: TGr_79 (flickr, CC)

---

12. Arnhem Central Station (2006/2015)

Masterplan design: UNStudio in collaboration with Cecil Balmond at Aurp AGU

Images credits
Sculptured Railway, Arnhem Station
source: Rob Oo,(flickr, CC)

A space for design: intersections and ambiguity

Looking back at the paradigmatic positions of the last century is possible to catch an important line of continuity with contemporary design positions, capable to trace a narrative regarding the relation between infrastructure and architecture from a disciplinary point of view. A common character that emerges from those readings is the progression of the typological research on *hybridization*, that still represents a fundamental aspect in contemporary design proposals for infrastructural nodes. Since the experimental design proposals of LC, infrastructure appears as autonomous element concurring in the construction of city. This interrelation strongly appears also in Second Modernism in which utopian urban systems meets the concept of formal finitude belonging to architectural sphere, as deeply investigated by the Italian research on Territorial Architecture. The Euralille project, as last paradigmatic manifesto, extremes this position. However if the interrelation between architecture and infrastructure represents a constant in the urban and architectural researches of the last century, today the richness of this heritage, in terms of spatial configurations, seems to be almost forgotten within a clear tendency to homologation. The contemporary design proposals for infrastructural nodes appear more and more similar ones to each others. Actors of investments, modalities of urban development, typologies functions and spatial characters are stigmatized as recognizable identikit more than an alphabet to play with. Independent both from the transport modalities itself, both from the specific context.

This tendency to homogeneity is, probably, the most significant aspect that characterize the contemporary research framework almost excluding, from the process and the design phases, a true interest to translate in spaces and forms what Van Eyck defines as the main character of transportation in the XXth century: «Today mobility is not any aspect of life in cities, but it is made of the very essence of human relationships.[16]»

Following this reflection, the contribution wants to outline a possible different position regarding the relation between Architecture and Infrastructure, not just based on functional or market needs. It is about the possibility to enhance the architectural research in spatial infrastructural-urban design that today seems almost excluded by the several ongoing interventions, but that needs to recapture new attention in order not to be stacked in retail simulacra or spatial cliché.

Beyond the experimental researches and design proposal about smart grids and the idea of infrastructure as a knowledge system that exchanges information with the surrounding environment, alternative approaches are emerging. The starting point relays on considering the meaning of infrastructure not as a structure lying beneath, physically ousted of any possibility of spatial nor semantic intersection with the city itself but, on the contrary, from considering the significance of infrastructure as something that stays 'in-between'.

«Etymologically, the term comes from the Latin *infra* and *structura*. *Infra* means under, which stay below; *structura* comes from *struere*, that means to build. Infrastructure literally means construction that is under, which is not seen (after all this is the interpretation that has emerged in recent decades; the infrastructure is something to hide beneath, which is better not to see). But *infra* in Latin has also the meaning of *in-between*: then we can understand it as construction that unites, that binds, that relates.[17]»

Even with different tones and interests these marginal researches express the need to recover a dialogue between infrastructure, mobility and city. Underlying the main reasons could be inspiring for further design perspectives.

Firstly, the co-existence of infrastructure and urban form, rather their interdependence becomes increasingly stronger in a social condition of more accessible mobility within European borders because of low cost trend. Indeed contemporary flows, at least within the old continent, are not based on stable migrations from one nation to another one, but exponentially is changing to an unfixed movement that enlighten the acquisition of an amplified geographic field of actions. This fact is not only understandable due to the ongoing project for a common infrastructural network[18] but to a new social status of European community, visible both on the macroscopic scale of the national territories and on that microscopic one of urban/local flows. The second reason, even more cumbersome, is that new technologies are radically changing transport modalities through self driven vehicles, electric hydrogen automobiles and on the incremental use of public transport to replace private one. Shortly, broader political and technological frameworks are transforming, in an accelerated present, the reasons *for* and *of* infrastructures, while these are still designed and intended as belonging to the common imagery of the smoky industrial city: dirty, polluting, noisy. All characters that envisioned infrastructure as barrier gradually relegating it, within a century of negotiations, to a definitive disconnection from the urban scene.

Today diverse experimental design proposals bind the infrastructural issue to the emerging urgencies that address both the social, the ecological and the spatial aspects of the future status of urban matter. Among them an important issue regards the need for the contemporary city for vertical stratification due to the complexity of functions and mobility pattern. However the risk that lies behind relates to the implicit possibility of social exclusion, which must be otherwise prevented. A well known example is, the project for the *High Line* in New York[19], regarding the reuse and the recycle of infrastructure through innovative bottom up actions that reopen to the large community an abandoned space inviting to the reappropriation of the urban space as common ground experience, it addresses again a social value to the infrastructure as element deeply embedded in the context.

Another emerging urgency is to reactivate the potential of infrastructural corridors, going beyond the landscape urbanism charging them with ecological values. The consciousness, indeed, is to regain a more liveable condition in metropolitan areas also preventing big climate changes. The italian team of Secchi and Viganò recall a new morphology for 'porous infrastructures'[20], using the concept of connectivity also for the green and blue corridors without escaping the figurativeness of infrastructural presences, but merging them in an innovative scenario. The team also won the important planning competition of *Grand Paris Consultation International sur l'avenir de la metropole parisienne*[21], where ten invited teams were asked to imagine the future of the french metropolis. Similarly to the ecological approach of Secchi and Viganò proposal, multilayered metropolitan ecological infrastructures have been hypothesized by the team 'Rogers Stirk harbour & Partners'. The proposal addresses the construction of 'Paris atop Paris', transforming and densifying unused or underused existing railways frames. Above these corridors, a system of multifunctional ecological armatures have been imagined. As linear platforms organized on multiple levels, they host mobility infrastructures together with social facilities and services, spaces for waste recycling, solar energy production and food production.

These research trajectories suggest new images for the future urban systems that associate infrastructures to vectors of energy transition within a broader concept of metabolism in which cities and metropolitan area contribute in a positive way to the overall environmental balance. The emerging figures of energetic backbones, together with the rediscover of their social values, deeply involve a spatial character as needed for envisioning future infrastructures, not anymore disconnected from urban form but on the contrary integrated in it. In that perspective a sort of *spatial interference* between city and infrastructure is again reclaimed. So that maybe in the coming years we will look for different modalities of morphological interference, reopening the current divided plans between cities and infrastructure. Moving further down the ground floor of the city, uncovering old subway lines and creating artificial parks in existing infrastructural plinths of interchanges and stations. The urgency, indeed, consists of associating one more time, but with different interests, the architectural research together with the advanced technologies of mobility, diverging from the described contemporary morphotypes and looking for new figures of intersection between infrastructure and urban form. What will probably happen is that we will have to rediscover a balance and a new dialogue between them, that goes from the current 'aut/aut' condition to a 'tertium dabatur'[22], a third way based on spatial, social and ecological intersection, that enlightens ambiguity as main tool for the renewal of the architectural linguistic codes.

1. The men who first drew a road between two places carried out one of the most important achievements. They could have come and gone between the two, so to make them unified, but only when they imprinted on the surface of the earth the road, those places were united objectively, the will had become Form of things, form that was offered to the will for each repetition without depending on its frequency or scarcity. In G. Simmel(1909), 'Brücke und Tür'. Der Tag; ed. it: G. Simmel, 'Ponte e Porta' in Cacciari M.; Perucchi, L. ed. (1970). *G. Simmel. Saggi di Estetica*. Padova: Cedam, p. 6

2. Partly developed in Berlingieri, F. (2013). State Transitions: Infrastructure and Urban Form in XXI th century. *Studio*, 4, p. 22-29.

3. Sitte, C. (1889). *Der Städtebau nach seinen künstlerischen grundsätzen*. Vienna: Graeser; ed. it: Sitte, C. (1981). *L'arte di costruire le città: l'urbanistica secondo i suoi fondamenti artistici*. Milano: Jaca Books, p.30-35.

4. Le Corbusier (1925). *Urbanisme*. Paris: G. Grés et Cieed. it.: Le Corbusier (1967) .*Urbanistica*. Milano: Il Saggiatore, p. 110.

5. Venturi, R. (1966). *Complexity and Contradiction in Architecture*. New York, The Museum of Modern Art; ed. it.: Venturi R. (1980). *Complessità e contraddizioni nell'architettura*. Bari, Ed. Dedalo, pp. 42,43.

6. About the history of the project and development phases: http://www. hafencity.com

7. For the ongoing projects on the redevelopment of harbour areas in Helsinki see: http://en.uuttahelsinkia.fi/

8. Lucan, J. (1991). *OMA-Rem Koolhaas 1970-1990*. New York: Princeton Architectural Press, pp. 118-126.

9. In botany, shape and particular size, devoid of taxonomic value, which can be taken from a plant species in response to particular environmental factors. A portion of the urban area that it has several characters among those closest to the particular combination of the constituent morphological elements: it is widely defined by localized character. *Morfotipo*. Treccani on line, (2017), www.treccani.it.

10. Privileggio, N. (2006). Contesto. In Purini, F. ed. (2006). *La città nuova Italia-y 2026, Biennale di Architettura Padiglione Italia*. Venezia: Marsilio Editore, p. 347.

11. Regarding the development phases see http://www.west8.nl/projects/madrid_rio/

12. Regarding the ongoing development of the project, it can

be observed on the project management website: http://www.a2maastricht.nl/nl/plan/groeneloper.aspx

13. Shannon, K.; Smets, M.(2010). *The Landscape of Contemporary Infrastructures*. Rotterdam: Nai Publishers, pp.68-90.

14. More informations can be found on the official website of the project: http://www.valenciaparquecentral.es/

15. Berlingieri, F.; Triggianese, M.(2014). Intermodal Nodes for the European Metropolis:Amsterdam Zuidas as EURandstad's gate. *Advanced Engineering Forum* (AEF) International journal, 29. 16. Van Eyck, A. (1962) *Passi verso una disciplina configurativa*. In Biraghi, M.; Damiani, G.; ed (2009) *Le parole dell'architettura. Un'antologia di testi teorici e critici: 1945-2000*. Einaudi, Torino, pp. 75-99.

17. Pavia, R. (2005). *Le paure dell'urbanistica*. Roma: Meltemi Babele, p.111.

18. For the Trans-European Network (TEN-T) project see: https://ec.europa.eu/transport/themes/infrastructure_en.

19. For the ongoing development of the project see the official website: www.thehighline.org.

20. Secchi, B.; Viganò, P. (2011). *La ville porouse*. Genéve: Editions MetisPresses, pp. 19-22.

21. For the eleven teams selected for the Grand Paris consultations (2008) and the design results see: www.ateliergrandparis.fr/aigp/conseil/consultation2008.php

22. The term 'tertium dabatur' is a latin language construct that means the possibility of a third alternative.

The construction of a stacked two layer tunnel that crosses below the Maastricht's urban center, grows to a length of 2.3 kilometers, will replace the fast lanes of road traffic with a cycle-pedestrian promenade, the green ribbon, delimited by trees and roads for the local traffic flows. The project involves, with the completion of the new underground infrastructure, the renovation of some areas along the route through a new urban scene made by residential buildings.

13. A2 Avenue, De Groene Loper Maastricht (2009/2026)

Masterplan design: Avenue2 Consortium: Ballast Nedam, Strukton, ARCADIS Nederland, West 8 Urban Design & Landscape Architecture, Humblé Architecten, dGmR, Bex* Communications.

Images credits
Maastricht, A2 avenue.
source: Kleon3 (wikicommons, CC)

14. Tiburtina Train Station Roma (2008/2011 Execution Phase)

Masterplan design: ABDR Architetti Associati

Images credits
New Tiburtina #2
source: Giorgio Minga (panoramio, CC)

15. Confluence Railway Bypass Lyon (2003/2016 On Going)

Masterplan design: Herzog and De Meuron architects (zac2); MVRDV, P.Gautier, M.Gautrand, ECDM e Erik van Egeraat, West 8 (Le Monilith); Jakob + Macfarlane Architects (Cube orange); M. Fuksas (Ilot B); Kengo Kuma (Ilot P)

Images credits
Confluences, Marina (Lyon)
source: jeangui111 (flickr, CC)

Architectural perspectives on Infrastructures and City; three accounts

Roberto Cavallo

Infrastructures and City: spatial contradictions
Contemporary urban areas are more and more confronted with the urgency of accommodating complicated and specific infrastructural solutions in order to satisfy the current demands of an increasingly complex society. In the meantime, while urban areas are working on new infrastructures, the continuous modernization and update of all types of requirements, the reorganization, the reconversion or the substitution of existing infrastructures ask very frequently for engineering and design solutions that are not always able to cope with the contemporary urban conditions. Indeed, particularly in the Western European context and from a spatial viewpoint, the city seems curiously to be almost incompatible with the presence of infrastructures. However, and without doubt, infrastructures have always been primary elements of the city. In fact, all processes of urbanization throughout history arise from the presence of traffic nodes where the interchange of people and goods can take place. These conditions created a natural interaction, and quite often a direct relationship, among infrastructures, the location where they are placed and the making of buildings. In addition, certain kinds of infrastructures are able to combine more than one mode of traffic, such as roads that are able to join together vehicular and pedestrian circulation, facilitating accessibility, development and transformation of urban areas. As Kevin Lynch already suggested in his famous 1960 book *Image of City*, and many others embraced, infrastructures are fundamental elements characterizing the city and its image. However, reversing the terms, many stereotypical ideas about the city assume at least contradictory positions towards infrastructures, accounting them often as barrier, as disturbing elements and even as alien to the city.

It is with this split in mind that we should consider this problematic in contemporary urban areas. Today, in the 21st century, the necessity of improving public transportation networks as an alternative to congested vehicular traffic, together with the urgency of developing environmentally friendly mobility solutions, poses very challenging prospects onto the current and future coexistence of infrastructures and city. In addition, there is already an existing urban condition to be considered in which infrastructures are entangled with the city and often act as physical barriers. Therefore academics as well as practitioners should study much deeply the various facets of the relationship between infrastructures and the physical layout as well as the functioning mechanisms of the city. Unfortunately, and despite all efforts, logic and management of large-scale infrastructure networks keep avoiding the issue of their spatial specificity missing the link with operative architectural strategies.

Infrastructures and City: unstable entanglement
An interesting perspective about contemporary infrastructures is the one given by Bernardo Secchi. In his article *Figure della mobilità*[1], he is rightly pointing out the multidimensional impact of infrastructures on contemporary life, questioning at the same time the role of designers within this scope:

«To move persons, things, energy and information, images and ideas, stored in increasingly sophisticated and miniaturized repositories of matter and memory, to utilize the time of movement and stillness to transform them, giving them new identity, roles, meanings and status, to construct the concrete physical and institutional infrastructures of mobility, or what permits and encourages movement and circulation, become a primary task of modern design».

According to Secchi's position, we should accept the inevitable interdependence between contemporary life – and not only urban – and infrastructures as a condition that needs to be envisaged on different scale levels. Elaborating further on the matter Secchi argues that

«it has often been said, and not without reason, that the solutions provided case by case to problems of mobility and circulation of things, people and ideas, are responsible to a great extent for the change, in the modern era, of the occidental cities and territories, of their role, their size and form».[2]

Moreover, Secchi stresses that this condition of interdependency between infrastructures and urban areas is mutual as well as cyclical:

«these changes, in turn, are laying at the origin of a constantly growing demand for mobility. Throughout the modern era, the infrastructure of mobility, on the one hand, and the form, role and size of the city and territory, on the other, seem to pursue each other in an eternal state of instability».[3]

Reading this part of Secchi's essay makes again very clear that although infrastructures -particularly the one concerning mobility- and cities are tightly interwoven, their mutual relationship is characterized by a constant state of instability. In fact, probably due to their heterogeneous natures and the involvement of too many and sometimes contrasting factors, it has been persistently very difficult to synchronize and harmonize infrastructures with the city. It is for these reasons that looking at this problematic from an architectural viewpoint, instability expresses very well the spatial condition of infrastructures in urban areas.

As matter of fact, the interesting but probably also striking fact about infrastructures is that they are subject to quick changes. It is in the nineteenth century, with the advent of the Industrial Revolution, that the problem of traffic becomes a pivotal issue for the city. The increasing number of inhabitants along with the transformation and growth of the city on the one hand, and the technological possibilities on the other, have significant consequences on traffic infrastructures and the way they interact with the city. It is exactly in this period that traffic infrastructures started to need their own accommodation in the city, not only in terms of space but ultimately also in terms of buildings. Up to the preindustrial period, overland urban traffic was mainly confined to the use of stagecoaches. Although centrally located in the city, the stagecoach depots were often housed on the ground floor of the existing urban fabric. In terms of architecture, this type of transportation required nothing new, as the depots were fully integrated in the existing buildings and their presence was not distinguishable in the surrounding urban fabric. Even when the horse-omnibus-on-track took the place of stagecoaches, there was still no need for other building accommodations. The first great change came with the construction of railroads. The railroad depots and stations had to vary from the stagecoaches depots simply because the functioning of train and railway track was different compared to the one of highway and street. However, it is remarkable that even decades after its advent, the railway, and notably the station, was not considered to be part of the city. The railroad often stopped at the edge of urban areas and was regarded for years as an alien threatening the beauty of the historical city. Nevertheless, these new urban conditions triggered the interest of several artists and inspired important avan-garde movements like the futurism.

It is in this context that railway stations, and later railway viaducts and bridges, were labelled mere utilitarian buildings, spatially and architecturally too 'unstable' for the city. Not being assimilated by the city as fully-fledged elements, the railroad buildings paradoxically represented the perfect ground for experimenting and applying new construction techniques using steel and concrete. In this way the transportation on track developed its own outward expression, but not as result of a well developed architectural thinking or as a strategy aiming at integrating infrastructures and city. Only the reception building of representative stations was erected out of stone, explicitly showing the need for a connection with the rest of the city, although primarily only in terms of appearance. According to this practice, many railways have been built in the past without considering their integration into the surrounding (urban) environment. On top of this, stations as well as railway yards, due to the

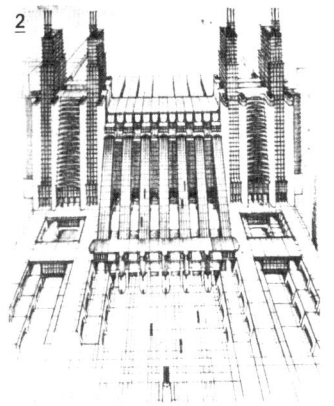 

expansion of cities and the rapid developments around railway terminals, ended up being completely enclosed by urban fabric, giving rise to spatial disconnection as well as fragmentation, commonly visible in phenomena like ribbon developments and fringe belts.[4]

After the railways, first personalized car traffic and later public buses showed up in the city. Motorized traffic required many modifications and adaptations in terms of urban space. Besides the transformation and the reorganization of public areas and streets, new parking zones and new terminal buildings were needed to support the new type of traffic. Along with the railway stations, a new family of utilitarian buildings started to play an important role in the city. Consequently, bus terminals, parking and garage buildings, flyovers, bridges or other types of traffic buildings needed their own spatial solutions. Nevertheless, although crucial for traffic, those buildings kept a marginal role as far as architecture is concerned. The need of standardisation and the technical performances, controlled and worked out by the engineer, were considered far more important than the appearance and the assimilation in the urban landscape. Although main railway stations, large bus stations, or centrally located parking garages were sometimes commissioned to architects, infrastructures and city maintained their unsynchronized relationship and instability, particularly in terms of mutual spatial integration. Therefore, in the light of these problems and constraints, there is still a strong need of continuing the search for new perspectives and possibilities envisioning the coexistence of city and infrastructure.

This unavoidable and unstable relationship should be at the same time a great challenge for architecture; to grasp the right spirit and understand the proper attitude we should again look to some great historical examples. Jumping few centuries back, on top of the list I would certainly put the *Vasarian Corridor* designed and executed in 1565 in the Florence of the Renaissance.[5] This very known project was commissioned by Cosimo 1th de Medici and came from the hand of Giorgio Vasari. The corridor, nowadays partly integrated in the famous Uffizi museum, was in fact a one kilometre elevated private route created to give opportunity to the duke and his family to move freely and safely from their residence (Palazzo Pitti) to the government palace (Palazzo Vecchio). The project was far from being easy as the route had to be juxtaposed on several historical buildings, trespassing basically the very heart of Florence. The corridor needed even to cross the river Arno; the solution foresaw a second layer added to the existing bridge Ponte Vecchio. The commission was crazy for that time but Vasari, with an extreme care for the integration of the new intervention with the existing urban surrounding, realised in only 5 months time this fantastic project, an unforgettable chapter in the history of infrastructures as well as of hybrid buildings.

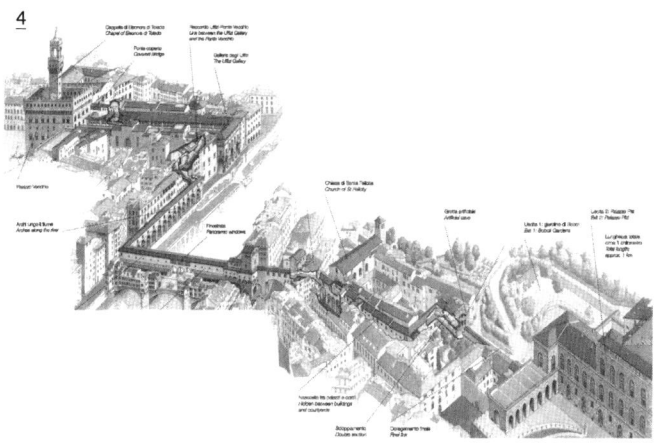

4

5

Infrastructure and city: does architecture matter?
Architects 'are not the technicians or engineers of the three great variables – territory, communications and speed. These escape the domain of the architects.'⁶. This is what Michel Foucault said in 1982 during an interview with Paul Rabinow. While recognizing that architecture does not play always a pivotal role, particularly if taking into consideration specific technical facets, accepting its total marginalization in the above mentioned discussion feels extremely inappropriate. If it's true that the design of bridges, highways, canals, harbours, aqueducts, railroads and so on, as products of mainly engineering work, does not primary need the involvement of architects, it is then at the other end also legitimate to emphasize the importance of managing the impact of these complex realizations in terms of their spatial performance and their assimilation in the urban territory. This is likely to be the domain of architecture.

The tremendous transformation of city and territory by the increasing speed of 'urban flows' needs, at least in spatial terms, to be envisaged, needs the involvement of architects and designers at different scale levels. One of the issues constantly deserving attention is that after years of coexistence, infrastructure buildings are also somehow integrated into the city and become an important part of its image. To make them survive continuous changes is not always possible but in may cases worth a try. Another important matter is the presence of several kinds of infrastructures in the city and their great influence on the way other buildings in the surrounding areas are designed or transformed. The interaction of these buildings with infrastructures is often the leading architectural theme of these interventions. Infrastructures are often superimposed on the city, generating interesting situations where the contrast between built and unbuilt spaces requires specific architectural solutions. Herein lay most challenges for designers, particularly towards the search for new solutions in transforming urban infrastructures. Ultimately, only by actively engaging in the thinking, in the designing and in the making, as well as participating in the debate (and not only the academic one) will architects be able to effectively claim a role in the spatial transformations of both infrastructures and cities.

In this framework there is a strong need of considering the different scale levels involved in the topic and, more specifically, the interference between these scales. A very important matter is the intertwining of the identity or memory traces, related to a specific urban area on different scale levels, with the infrastructural dynamics. Within this perspective, specific historical and socioeconomic knowledge play an important role, particularly in understanding the mutations that took place in these particular urban areas. In other words, to be able to transform them, it is essential to understand the place specificity connotations of infrastructures. Some of the topical questions would than regard the role of the network, the meaning of dialectics and conflicts between old and new or the problem of measuring performance and effectiveness in terms of space of both developments and transformations in urban areas.

Many issues turned on by transforming infrastructures are often characterized by similar trends. However, it is impossible to act following a general strategy of intervention. The relationship between the singular (infrastructural) building, the problematic of the surrounding urban area and the changing infrastructures are in every single case too specific and complicated to allow general operational conclusions. At the other end, we can all agree that the performance of infrastructures must also be measured in terms of their spatial assimilation. For these reasons, and in order to properly contribute to the on going and future discussions, there will be a persistent need of pursuing further studies about the interrelations between infrastructure and city.

1. Secchi, B. (2005). Figure della mobilità. Casabella, 739-740, p. 80-83.

2. Ibidem, p.82.

3. Ibidem, p.83.

4. For a detailed explanation about fringe belts, see von der Dollen, B. A historical-geographical perspective on urban fringe-belt phenomena. Slater, T.R. (1990) *The built form of Western cities. Essays for M.R.G.Conzen on the occasion of his eightieth birthday.* Leicester: Leicester University Press, p. 319.

5. For more information look at the book: Mandelli, E. (2005). *I percorsi del Principe a Firenze. Rilievo integrato tra conoscenza e lettura critica.* Florence: Alinea.

6. Rabinow, P. (1984). *Space, Knowledge and Power, The Foucault Reader interview with Michel Foucault*, translated by Christian Hubert. New York: Pantheon, p. 244.

1. MARIO SIRONI, 1922. Suburbs.
source: Agnoldomenico Pica, *Mario Sironi*. (Milan: Edizioni Del Milione), 1955.

2. Drawing. The elevated sidewalk. Front cover of the magazine SCIENTIFIC AMERICAN, July 26th 1913.
source: Jean Castex, Chicago 1910-1930 *Le chantier de ville moderne.* (Paris: De la Villette), 2010.

3. Drawing. Milan Central Station project by Antonio Sant'Elia, 1914.
source: Source: Reyner BaΩnham, Megastructure; urban futures of the recent past. (New York: Harper & Row), 1976.

4. Drawing. Overview of the Vasarian Corridor.
source: http://michelangelobuonarrotietornato.com/tag/corridoio-vasariano/

5. Photograph of part of the Vasarian Corridor with the Ponte Vecchio in the background
source: http://www.turismo.intoscana.it/allthingstuscany/tuscanyarts/vasari-exhibit-uffizi/

Bibliography

1. CRITICISM AND THEORY IN URBAN STUDIES

1.1. MODERNISM (1890/1960)

AA.VV. (2010). *LCBOG. Le Corbusier en Bogotà 1947-1951*. Bogota: Ediciones Uniandes

Benevolo, L. (1964). *Le origini dell'urbanistica moderna*. Bari: Editori Laterza

Benjamin, W. (1928). *Einbahnstraße*. Berlin: Rowohlt (Ed.It.: (1997). *Strada a senso unico. Scritti 1926-1927*. Torino: Giulio Einaudi Editore

Benjamin, W. (Ed. It. 2007). *I "passages" di Parigi*. Torino: Giulio Einaudi Editore

Benjamin, W. (Ed. It. 2007). *Immagini di città*. Torino: Giulio Einaudi Editore

Biraghi, M.; **Damiani**, G. (2009). *Le parole dell'architettura. Un'antologia di testi teorici e critici: 1945-2000*. Torino: Giulio Einaudi Editore

Bonillo, J.L. (ed) (2012). *Le Corbusier Visions d'Alger*. Fondation Le Corbusier. Paris: La Villette

Cacciari, M. (1973). *Metropolis*. Roma: Officina

Casabella, (1987). Le Corbusier, n. 531-532

Garnier, T. (1917). *Une Cité industrielle. Etude pour la construction des villes*. (Ed. It.: (1985). *Architetture per la città industriale*. Roma: Officina Edizioni)

Gedion, S. (1941). *Space, Time, Architecture. The Growth of a new tradition*. (Ed. It.: (1954). *Spazio tempo e architettura, lo sviluppo di una nuova tradizione*. Milano: Hoepli)

Ghersi, F. (2008). *Scritti sulla Modernità*. Cannitello: Biblioteca del Cenide

Hilberseimer, L. (1927). *Groszstadt Architektur*. (Ed. It.: (1981). *L'architettura delle grandi città*. Napoli: Edizioni Clean)

Le Corbusier (1925). *Urbanisme*. (Ed. it.: (1967).*Urbanistica*. Milano:Il Saggiatore)

Le Corbusier (1946). *Manière de penser l'urbanisme*. (Ed. It.: (1972 IV ed.). *Maniera di pensare l'urbanistica*. Bari: Editori Laterza)

Le Corbusier, (1941). *Sur Les Quatre Routes*. Paris: Editions Gallimard

Lipstadt, H; **Mendelsohn**, H. (1993). Philosophy, History and Autobiography: Manfredo Tafuri and the "Unsurpassed Lesson" of Le Corbusier. *Assemblage*, n. 22

Mittner, D. (2003). *Le città di fondazione nel Novecento*. Torino: Testo&Immagine

Mumford, L. (1958). *The Highway and the city*. New York: Harcourt, Brace & World.

Pouliot, H. (2011). 'Machines for living' Reflections on Le Corbusier's Plan Obus (Algiers) & Unité d'Habitation (Marseilles). *SHIFT* Graduate Journal of Visual and Material Culture, n. 4.

Rykwert, J. (2003). *La seduzione del luogo. Storia e futuro della città*. Torino: Giulio Einaudi Editore

Simmel, G. (1903). *Die Großstädte und das Geistesleben*. (Ed. It.: (1996, II ed.). *La metropoli e la vita dello spirito*. Roma: Armando Editore)

Sorya y Mata, A. (1882). *La ciudad lineal*. (Ed. It.: (1968). *La città lineare e altri scritti, 1894-1905*. Milano: Il Saggiatore)

Wright, F.L. (1932).*The disappearing city*. New York: W.F. Payson ed. (Ed. It.: (1991). *La città vivente*. Torino:Einaudi)

1.2. MEGASTRUCTURES AND "ARCHITETTURA TERRITORIALE" (1960/1980)

Banham, R. (1976). *Megastructures: urban future of the recent past*. (Ed. It.: (1980). *Megastrutture: le tentazioni dell'architettura*. Bari: Laterza Editori)

Casabella (1991). Il disegno del paesaggio italiano, n.575-576

Crispolti, E. (1979). *Immaginazione megastrutturale dal futurismo ad oggi*. Venezia: Marsilio Editore

Corboz, A. (1989). Il territorio come palinsesto. *Casabella*, n. 516

Frampton, K. (1999). *Megaform as Urban Landscape*, The Raoul Wallenberg Lecture. Brian Carter: New York (Ed. It.: (2002). Megaforma come paesaggio urbano. *Ottagono*, n.153)

Gregotti, V. (1967). *Il territorio dell'architettura*. Bologna: Feltrinelli

Gregotti, V. (2012) «Territori delle Infrastrutture». In Ferlenga, A.; Albrecht, B.; Biraghi, M. (2012) *L'Architettura del Mondo. Infrastrutture, mobilità, nuovi paesaggi*. Catalogo della Mostra alla Triennale di Milano. Firenze: Editrice Compositori

Gregotti, V. (1989). La strada: tracciato e manufatto. *Casabella*, n. 553-554

Kolson, K. (2001). *Big plans: the allure and the folly of urban design*. Baltimore: the J. Hopkins University Press

Purini, F. (1976). *Luogo e Progetto*. Roma: Magma Editrice

Quaroni, L. (1967). *La Torre di Babele*. Venezia: Marsilio Editore

Quaroni, L. (1981). *La città fisica*. Roma: Laterza Editore

Rogers, E.N. (1968). *Editoriali di architettura*. Torino: Einaudi

Rossi, A. (1966). *L'architettura della città*. Padova: Marsilio Editore

Rossi, A. (1975). *Scritti scelti sull'architettura e la città*. Torino: Città Studi Edizioni

Samonà, G. (1959). *L'urbanistica e l'avvenire della città degli stati europei*. Roma: Laterza Editore

Samonà, G. (1964). *La città territorio*. Bari: De Donato Editore

Smithson, A.(1964). *Team Ten Primer*. London: Rouledge

Tafuri, M. (1973). *Progetto e Utopia*. Bari: Laterza Editore

Tafuri, M.; **Penta**, B.L.L.(1976). *Architecture and utopia*. Cambridge: Mit Press

1.3. POSTMODERN AND CONTEMPORARY (1980/2012)

Appleyard, D.; Lynch, K.; Myer, J. (1964). *The view from the Road*. Cambridge: Mit Press.

Ascher, F. (1995). *Metapolis ou l'avenir des villes*. Paris: O. Jacobs

Banham, R. (2004). *Architettura della seconda età della macchina*. Milano: Electa

Baudrillard, J. (1968). *Le sisteme d'objects*. (Ed. It.: (2006). il sistema degli oggetti. Milano: Bompiani)

Cacciari, M. (1997). *L'Arcipelago*. Milano: Adelphi

Cacciari, M. (2004). *La città*. Verrucchio: Pazzini

Casabella (1989). Sulla Strada, n.553-554

Casabella (1991). Il disegno del paesaggio italiano, n. 575-576

Choay, F. (1992). *L'orizzonte del posturbano*. Roma: Officina Edizioni

Choay, F. (2000). *La città. Utopie e realtà*. Torino: Einaudi

Clèment, G. (2006), *Il manifesto del Terzo Paesaggio*. Macerata: Quodlibet

De Fusco, R. (2005). *Architettura come mass medium*. Bari: Dedalo Edizioni

Foucault, M. (2001). *Spazi altri. I luoghi delle etorotopie*. Milano: Mimesis

Geddes, P. (1970). *Città in evoluzione*. Milano: Il Saggiatore

Grahame, S. D. (2005). *Recombinant Urbanism. Conceptual modelling in Architecture Urban Design and City Theory.* London: Wiley Academy

Habermas, J. (1998). *Die Postnationale Konstellation.* Frankfurt a/M: Suhrkamp Verlag

Hays, M. (2000). *Architecture Theory since 1968.* Cambridge, London: Mit Press

Hénard, E. (1982). *Alle origini dell'urbanistica: la costruzione della metropoli.* Padova: Marsilio Editore

Holl, S. (1991). *Edge of a City.* New York: Pamphlet Architecture

Koolhaas, R.; Boeri, S.; Kwinter, S.; Tazi, N.; Obrist, H.; editors (2001). *Mutations.* Barcelona: Actar

Koolhaas, R. (2006). *Junkspace. Per un ripensamento radicale dello spazio urbano.* Macerata: Quodlibet

Lucan, J. (1991). OMA-Rem Koolhaas, Architecture 1970-1990. New York: Princeton Architectural Press

Lynch, K. (1960). *The image of the city.* Cambridge: Mit Press

Mazzeri, C. (2002). Bernardo Secchi, Carlo Olmo, Stefano Boeri, Marco De Michelisi, Oriol Bohigas, Vittorio Gregotti, *La città europea del XXI secolo. Lezioni di storia urbana.* Milano: Skira

Neri, G.; Petranzan, M. (2009). *Franco Purini. La città uguale. Scritti scelti sulla città e il progetto urbano dal 1966 al 2004.* Padova: Il Poligrafo

Perulli, P. (2009). *Visioni di città. Le forme del mondo spaziale.* Torino: Einaudi

Prigogine I.; **Stengers** I. (1981). *La nuova alleanza.* Torino: Einaudi

Rowe, C.; **Koetter**, G (1978). *Collage City.* London: Routledge

Secchi, B. (2008). *La città nel XX secolo.* Roma: Laterza

Thermes, L. (2000). *Tempi e spazi: la città e il suo progetto nell'età posturbana.* Roma: Diagonale Editrice

Ungers, O.M.; Vieths, S. (1997). *La città dialettica.* Milano: Skira

Venturi, R.; **Scott Brown**, D. (1972), Learning from Las Vegas. NY: The MIT press

Vidler, A. (1977). The third typology. *Oppositions*, n. 7

Vidler, A. (2000). *Warped space. Art, architecture and anxiety in modern culture.* NY: The Mitt Press (Ed. It.: (2009). *La deformazione dello spazio.* Milano: Postmediabooks)

2. CONTEMPORARY RESEARCH ON INFRASTRUCTURE AND CITY

Area (2005), n. 79

Casabella (1993), n. 597-598

AA.VV. (2009), *Il paesaggio e le infrastrutture.* Brescia: La Rosa

Anderson, S. (1982) *Strade.* Bari: Dedalo Edizioni

Boeri, S.; Multiplicity editors (2003). *USE: Uncertain States of Europe.* Milano: Skira

Brouer, J.; Mulder, A.; Martz, L. (2002). *Transurbanism.* Rotterdam: Nai Publisher

Calabrese, L. M. (2004). *Reweaving UMA, urbanism mobility architecture.* Rotterdam : PhD TU Delft, Optima grafische communicatie

Castels, M. (2004). *La città delle reti.* Padova: Marsilio

Clementi, A.; **Cannavò**, P. (2003), *Infrascape. Infrastrutture e paesaggio.* Firenze: Mandragora

Corboz, A. (1998). *Ordine Sparso.* Milano: Franco Angeli Editore

Crotti, S. (1986). Strade. Frontiere interne della trasformazione urbana. *Urbanistica*, n. 83

Desideri, P.; **Ilardi**, M. (1997). *Attraversamenti. I nuovi territori dello spazio pubblico*. Milano: Costa&Nolan

De Solà Morales, I. (2001). Territori. *Lotus*, n. 110

Desvigne, M.; **Dalnoky**, C. (1995). Trasformazioni indotte. *Lotus International*, n. 87

Eaton, R.(2002). *Ideal Cities, Utopianism and the (Un)built Environment*. London: Thames &Hudson ltd.

Graham, S.; **Marvin**, S. (2002). *Splintering Urbanism. Networked infrastructures, technological mobilities and urban conditions*. London, New York: Routledge

Gregotti, V (1999). *Identità e crisi dell'architettura europea*. Torino: Einaudi

Gregotti, V. (2011). *Architettura e postmetropoli*. Torino: Einaudi

Harvey, D. (1997). *L'esperienza urbana. Metropoli e trasformazioni sociali*. Milano: Il Saggiatore

Hauck, T.; **Keller**, R.; **Kleinkort**, V.; editors (2011). *Infrastructural Urbanism. Addressing the In-between*. Berlin: Dom Publisher

Houben, F.; **Calabrese**, L.M. (2003). *Mobility: a room with a view*. Rotterdam: Nai Publishers

Hoete, A. (2003). *Roam: reader on aesthetics of mobility*. New York: Black dog Publishing

Ilardi, M. (2002). *In nome della strada*. Roma: Meltemi

Ingersoll, R. (2004). *Sprawltown*. Roma: Meltemi Editore

Ingersoll, R. (2005). Jumpcut urbanism. L'estetica dell'ambiente motorizzato. *Parametro*, n.256

Isola, A. (2002) *Forme insediative e infrastrutture. Procedure, criteri e metodi per il progetto*. Venezia: Marsilio Editore

L'Arca (2000). Movimento, n.145

Lassus, B. (1998), *The Landscape Approach*. Philadelphia: University of Pennsylvania Press

Lassus, B. (2003), La rete autostradale e i nuovi valori paesaggistici. *T&C Trasporti e Cultura*, n. 6

Lassus, B. (1994), *Autoroute et paysage*. Parigi: Ed. Du Demi- Cercle

Lotus Navigator (2009). Infrastructures Landscape, n.139

Lotus Navigator (2003). Il paesaggio delle freeway, n.7

Lynch, K. (1964). *The view from the Road*. Cambridge: Mit Press

Maffioletti, S.; **Rocchetto**, S. (2002). *Infrastrutture e paesaggi contemporanei*. Padova: Il Poligrafo

Maffioletti, S. (2005). *Paesaggi delle infrastrutture*. Padova: Il Poligrafo

Maffioletti, S., **Sordina**, R. (2009). *Spazi, figure, paesaggi delle strade contemporanee*. Padova: Il Poligrafo

Marinoni, G. (2006). *Infrastrutture nel progetto urbano*. Milano: Franco Angeli

Marzot, N. (2011). Infrastrutture e reti. *XXI Secolo*, Treccani on line.

Micheletti, C., **Ponticelli**, M. (2003). *Nuove infrastrutture per nuovi paesaggi*. Milano: Skira

Morandi, M. (2003). *Progettare una strada. Progettare la città*. Firenze: Alinea Editrice

Moretti, A. (1996). *Le strade. Un progetto a molte dimensioni*. Milano: Franco Angeli editore

Mumford, L. (1958). *The highway and

the City. New York: Harcourt, Brace, & World

MVRDV (2003). *Five minute city. Architecture and (im)mobility*. Rotterdam: Episode Publisher

Nancy, J.L.(2002). *La città lontana*. Padova: Ombre corte

Pavia, R., (2003). Abitare tra le reti. *Piano Progetto Città*, n.19

Ponticelli, L.; **Micheletti**, C. (2003). *Nuove infrastrutture per nuovi paesaggi*. Milano: Skira

Privileggio, N. (2006). Infrastrutture, architettura: alcune precisazioni. In http: // www.arch'it/files

Privileggio, N. (2008). *La città come testo critico*. Milano: Franco Angeli Editore

Purini, F. (2005). Questioni di infrastrutture. *Casabella*, n. 739-740

Purini, F. (2003). La fine del viadotto. *Piano Progetto Città*, n.19

Quaderns (1997). Rethinking Mobility, n. 218

Rassegna (1991). Ponti abitati, n. 48

Ricci, M. (1996). *Figure della trasformazione*. Pescara: Ed'A

Richards, B.(2001). *Future Transport in Cities*. London: Spon Press

Rogers, R.(1997). *Cities for a small planet*. London: Faber and Faber limited

Rouillard, D.; **Prelorenzo**, C. (2009). *La metropole des infrastructures*. Paris: Picard

Rouillard, D. (2009). *Imaginaires d'infrastructure*. Paris: L'Harmattan

Secchi, B. (2005). Figure della mobilità. *Casabella*, n. 739-740

Secchi, B. (2005). Lo spessore della strada. *Casabella*, n. 739-740

Shannon, K.; Smets, M., editors (2010). *The Landscape of Contemporary Infrastructure*. Rotterdam: Nai Publishers

Sassen, S. (2002). *Global Networks, Linked Cities*. London: Routledge

Urbanistica Informazioni (2002). Infrastrutture e forme insediative, n.181

3. EUROPEAN IDENTITY IN CONTEMPORARY URBAN TRANSFORMATIONS

AA.VV. (2000), *Inserimento delle infrastrutture nel paesaggio francese*. Milano: Alinea

Andersson, H.; **Jorgensen**, G.; **Joye**, D.; **Ostendorf**, W., eds. (2001). *Change and Stability in Urban Europe. Form, quality and governance*. Ashgate: Aldershot

Avermaete, T. edited by (2009). On Territories. *Oase Journal*, n. 80

Bellicini, L. (1996). "Infrastrutture. Italia e Europa a confronto", in Clementi, A. (edited by), *Infrastrutture e piani urbanistici*, Quaderni blu 4. Roma: Fratelli Palombi Editori, Roma

Cacciari, M. (1994). *Geofilosofia dell'Europa*. Milano: Adelphi

Casabella (2002), n.695-696

Cavallo, R.; **Geerts**, F.; **Martin Blas**, S. (2006). "European infrastructures: identity and pragmatism introduction to the journal Dimensions" in *Building City Territory*. Venice: IUAV Venezia

Cavallo, R. (2004). 'Transformers of the European City', in François Claessens and Henk Engel (ed.), *OverHolland 1*. Amsterdam

Cavallo, R. (2005). 'Railway and transformation of the city: integrating research and design studies', in *EURAU 2005 - Considering space on a large scale*. Lille

Clementi, A.; **Dematteis**, G.; **Palermo**, P.C. (1996). *Le forme del territorio ita-*

liano. Temi e immagini del mutamento. Roma: Laterza

Bialasiewicz, L.; C. **Minca** (2005). Old Europe, New Europe: For a Geopolitics of Translation. *Area*, n.37

Dematteis, G.; **Governa**, F. (edited by) (2001). *Contesti locali e grandi infrastrutture. Politiche e progetti in Italia e in Europa*. Milano: Franco Angeli Editore

Derrida, J. (1991). *L'autre cap*. Paris: Éditions de Minuit. (translated by P.A. Brault and M.Naas as *The Other Heading: Reflections on Today's Europe*. Bloomington, IN.: Indiana University Press, 1992)

Di Giampietro, G. (1991). Strade a priorità ambientale. Progetti "minimalisti" in Danimarca e Olanda. *L'Arca*, n.18

Farinelli, F. (2003). *Geografia, un'introduzione ai modelli del mondo*. Torino: Einaudi

Gregotti, G. (1999). *Identità e crisi dell'architettura europea*. Torino: Einaudi

Karrer, F.; **Di Giampietro**, G. edited by (1993). *Il progetto di strade: una rassegna di esperienze*. Cosenza: Pellegrini

Karrer, F. (1995). *Effetti territoriali delle infrastrutture di trasporto*. Cosenza: Pellegrini

Kineo (1994). Arte sulle autostrade in Francia, n.3

Kineo (1995). Autostrade in Francia, n.9

Koolhaas, R. (1996) "Euralille", in AA.VV. *Sensori del futuro. L'architetto come sismografo. Sesta mostra internazionale di architettura della Biennale di Venezia*. Milano: Electa

Le Galès, P. (2000), *Cities in contemporary Europe*. Cambridge: Cambridge University Press. Lotus International (2000), n. 104

Purini, F.; **Marzot**, N.; **Sacchi**, L. edited by (2006). *La città nuova italia-y-26, invito a VEMA. La Biennale di Venezia, Il Padiglione Italiano alla 10. Mostra Internazionale di Architettura*. Bologna: Editrice Compositori

Smets, M. (2001). Il nuovo paesaggio delle infrastrutture in Europa. Lotus International, n.110

16

The redevelopment of the Railway Station Area, a real caesura in Valencia's city heart, is based on the underground tunnel of the railway arriving to the Central Station, because of the new high speed line construction. The general plan signs some focal points along the reconstruction of the avenida that will connect the South zone to the central urban areas. Along the new axis is located a linear park that converges in the area of the Parque Central, an old rail storage area, that will be the first city green lung.

17. Parque Central Valencia (2003/2026)

Masterplan design: Gustafson Porter architects; Borgos Pieper architects; Nova Ingeniería Project Management; Grupotec Engineers; Ove Arup & partners

Images credits
Parque central
source: El Pais

17. Port Mediterranee Marseille (1995/2013)

Masterplan design: EPAEM (l'Etablissement Public d'Aménagement d'Euroméditerranée)Norman Foster e Michel Desvigne; Zaha Hadid Architects (CMA CGM); 5+1AA (Docks); Rudy Ricciotti e Roland Carta (Mucem); Stefano Boeri (Città del Mediterraneo); M. Fuksas (Euromed Center); Kengo Kuma (Franc)

Images credits
Vue de Marseille
source: Jean-Pierre Dalbéra (flickr, CC)

18. Central Development Jätkäsaari Helsinki (2013/2026)

Redevelopment of former harbor area of central Helsinki

Images credits
Jätkäsaari housing construction
source: uuttahelsinkia.fi/jatkasaari

Published by
LISt Lab
info@listlab.eu
listlab.eu

Editorial Director
Alessandro Franceschini

Author
Fabrizia Berlingieri

Art Director, Graphic Design & Produzione
Blacklist Creative, BCN
blacklist-creative.com

ISBN 9788899854737

Printed and bound in European Union,
February 2018

All rights reserved
© of the edition LISt Lab;
© of the text the authors;
© of the images the authors.

Promotion and distribution in Italy
Messaggerie Libri, Spa, Milano,
Numero verde 800.804.900
assistenza.ordini@meli.it;

International promotion and distribution
ACC Book Distribution Ltd
Woodbridge, Suffolk, IP12 4SD, UK
sales@antique-acc.com

The Scientific Committee of the issues List
Eve Blau (Harvard GSD), Maurizio Carta (Università di Palermo), Alfredo Ramirez (Architectural Association London) Alberto Clementi (Università di Chieti), Alberto Cecchetto (Università di Venezia), Stefano De Martino (Università di Innsbruck), Corrado Diamantini (Università di Trento), Antonio De Rossi (Università di Torino), Franco Farinelli (Università di Bologna), Carlo Gasparrini (Università di Napoli), Manuel Gausa (Università di Genova), Giovanni Maciocco (Università di Sassari/Alghero), Antonio Paris (Università di Roma), Mosè Ricci (Università di Trento), Roger Riewe (Università di Graz), Pino Scaglione (Università di Trento).

LISt Lab is an editorial workshop, based in Europe, that works on contemporary issues. LISt Lab not only publishes, but also researches, proposes, promotes, produces, creates networks.

LISt Lab is a green company committed to respect the environment. Paper, ink, glues and all processings come from short supply chains and aim at limiting pollution. The print run of books and magazines is based on consumption patterns, thus preventing waste of paper and surpluses. LISt Lab aims at the responsibility of the authors and markets, towards the knowledge of a new publishing culture based on resource management.